SANGAM TAMILS

WITH SPECIAL REFERENCE TO PAṬṬINAPĀLAI

MJP
PUBLISHERS

SANGAM TAMILS

WITH SPECIAL REFERENCE TO PAṬṬINAPĀLAI

M. Thilakavathy

Associate Professor and Head,
Department of History Tourism and Travel Management,
Ethiraj College For Women,
Chennai.

MJP Publishers

Chennai New Delhi Tirunelveli

ISBN 978-81-8094-189-4

Printed and bound in India

MJP Publishers
No. 44 Nallathambi Street,
Triplicane,
Chennai 600 005

MJP 235

Publisher : J.C. Pillai

PREFACE

Dr.A.L.Basham, who was professor of Indian and South Asian Histories, University of London, pointed out that a critical investigation of the Sangam classics in Tamil had not been undertaken. The Department of Indian History, University of Madras, therefore undertook a critical study of the Tamil Sangam classics, from the view point of history. The study covered three Tamil classics, the Narrinai, the Kuruntogai and Ahananuru, all belongimg to the Aham group of Tamil Literature. Hence, I thought it is fit to cover the other Sangam classics of this group and chose to write on Pattinappalai written by the poet Uruttirangannanar .

Sangam literature comprises some of the oldest extant Tamil literature and deals with love, war, governance, trade and bereavement. Unfortunately, much of the Tamil literature belonging to the Sangam period has been lost. The literature currently available from this period is perhaps just a fraction of the wealth of material produced during (this) Golden Age of Tamil civilisation.

Many scholars both Indian and foreign have observed that Indians of the past, despite their high intellectually attainments, lacked the historic spirit.

However, Sangam classics of the early Tamils are an exception since it contains data of great historical value. These works play a great role in the study of ancient Sangam history. They provide authentic information on the socio-economic, political and religious conditions of the age. The earliest account of the Sangam appears in the Iraiyanar ahapparul (grammer of tamil poetry) which speaks of the three Sangams that existed for more that 9000 years and consisted of more than 8000 poets. Apparently, the accounts contained both facts and fiction. It is believed that literary works of the first two Sangams perished in a tsunami and that most of the texts that are available today are produced of the third Sangam.

The determination of the age the Sangam itself is rather difficult and the dates have always been a subject of great speculation.

According to Dr K.K.Pillai "The early Tamil classics known as the Sangam works are remarkably helpful in the reconstruction of history. The pen pictures provided by them are realistic for the most part, and therefore, though they do not constitute systematic history, they provide useful information on the political, social, economic and religious conditions of the age."

The Sangam literature consists of the eight anthologies called *Ettutogai* of short lyrics and the *Ten Idylls* known as *Pattupattu*. These works are broadly classified into two divisions' viz. . Puram works speaks about external matters like war and patronage of king, and Aham that speaks about love. Among the *TenIdylls, Porunararruppadai, Sirupanarruppadai, Perumbanarruppadai, Thirumurugarruppadai* and *Malaipadukadam* are poems on patrons, and *Mullaippattu, Nedulvadai, Kurinjippatu* and *Pattinappalai* are love poems while *Maduraikanchi* is a benedictory poem.

A Unique feature about puram poems is that they dealt with a situation in objective and in a realistic manner. The achievements of prominent rulers and the character of monarchy are the only data on political history that can be obtain from poems.

Patinenkilkanakku or the *Eighteen minor* works also find place in a Sangam classics the kural , another literary classic is assigned to the Sangam age.

Political History

The Pandyas, Cheras and Cholas and many minor chieftains ruled Tamil Nadu for over several centuries. References to the Pandyas kings are found in poems like *Maduraikkanchi*. The *Purananuru, Ahananuru, Kurunthogai, Narrinai* and the Epic *Silappadikaram* sing praises of the king Nedunchezian on his generosity, velour and Vedic sacrifices.

The data available on chola kings are commendable. Karikala one of the most famous kings of the Sangam Age is featured in the poem Pattinapalai. His exploits have also found mention in Purananuru and Porunararrupadai.

The only dynasty which can be fairly constructed with the aid of Tamil literature is that of Cheras. Padirrupattu concern themselves with the Chera kings.. The history of eight kings has been mentioned in Padirruppattu and clearly senguttuvan is the most outstanding personality. Like Karikalan, Senguttuvan also performed Vedic sacrifices and was a great warrior.

Details concerning the early Tamil kings their expeditions, pattern of military training and warfare are available from early literature. Impartial justice, promotion of economic well being and performances of religious rites and duties were considered important by the rulers. The Kural is the standing example and was declared 'the world's Bible' by scholars and people alike. It contains a systematic exposition of the responsibilities of an ideal king.

Socio- Religious Conditions

Purananuru and Pattupattu provide information about the social habit and custom of the age. Purananuru speaks about Pre Aryan caste and the Aryan fourfold classificationof the society. The women of the Sangam age were held in high respect and Pattupattu reveals that they enjoyed great personal freedom. Perumpanarupadai describes the participation of young girls and ladies in village festivals. Pattinappalai provides abundant data for the social historian, for example it mentions about the people habits it says Meat and Liquor were commonly used in the Sangam Age (Pattinappalai 108)

Silapathigaram one of the two great epic of the Sangam age provides information on the different forms of music and dance, and the various kinds of musical instruments there existed during this period.

Kurunji pattu mentions about the customs of women arranging their hair in five braids. *Madurai Kanchi* and *Pattinappalai* vividly portray the habits and customs of the Paradavas, the fisher fork in Neydal (one of the five natural divisions of the land described in the Sangam works).

Tolkappiyam, a great work on Tamil grammar contains religious beliefs and observances of the Sangam period. There is no invocation to god. It is clear that Sangam people believed in a supreme God and in a three- fold Trinity, very different from that of Aryans. Sangam age people worshipped Muruga and Korravai. Temples were built on hills for the worship of Muruga. The Thirumurugarrupadai, which was chronologically the last of the 'Pattupattu' was composed in reverence of lord Muruga. Later on, Muruga was identified with the Aryan god Karthikeya and Korravai to goddess Durga. Slowly a fusion of ideas and practices pertaining to religion started appearing. The period of twin Epics stand testimony to this change.

In respect of social position the Sangam works do not make a deliberate attempt at overrating the customs and manners, the institutions and the life of the people. Those were the days when there was no conscious effort glorifying one's own culture. Therefore the pen pictures and casual references provided by the poets of the Sangam age are refreshingly realistic.

Thus we find Sangam Literature has been valuable source of information for the construction of the history of the Sangam Age. With a little care and caution it is possible to narrate the events of the period in fair terms of accuracy for the sake of posterity.

In this work "Sangam Tamils With Special Reference To Paṭṭinapālai" an attempt has been made to provide the historical facts of the Sangam Age, objectively.

Note on Transliteration and Diacritical Marks – The system here adopted is the same as the Tamil Lexicon of the University of Madras, Vol.VI and p.LXVIII.

Tamil Alphabets and their English symbols with diacritical marks. Sanskrit words and the names of authors which have already found place in many works (e.g. Sangam, Raghava Iyengar) have been given in their familiar forms to avoid confusion.

I express my most sincere and grateful thanks to the Mr. Janarthanan of MJP Publishers for having kindly consented to publish this work.

ABBREVIATIONS

Ainkuru	...	Ainkurunuru
Akam	...	Akananuru
Cilampu	...	Cilappatlkaram
Cirupan	...	Cirupanarruppatai
Kali	...	Kalittokai
Kurun	...	Kuruntokai
Malai	...	Malaipatukatam
Mani	...	Manimekalai
Matural	...	Maturaikkanci
Mullai	...	Mullalppattu
Narri	...	Narrlnai
Netunal	...	Netunalvadai
Pari	...	Paripatal
Patirru	...	Patlrruppattu
Pattina	...	Pattinappalal
Perumpan	...	Perumpanarruppatal
Porunar	...	Porunararruppatai
Puram	...	Purananuru
Tol	...	Tolkappiyam

CONTENTS

Chapter I

THE AGE OF PAṬṬINAPĀLAI

Introduction

Paṭṭinappālai, a long lyric included in Pattupāṭṭu (the Ten Idylls) is one of the earliest extent Tamil classics of 'the Sangam Age'. The period of the Sangam age is now recognised by all scholars and historians as well to be the classical age of the Tamils parallel to the classical age of Greece and Rome.

M. Arokiaswami observes, "the classical age of the Tamils is not only by the consensus of learned opinion but also as proved by indisputable evidences, assigned to the first few centuries before and after the commencement of the Christian era. The literature produced by the Tamils of that age is known as the Sangam Literature".[1] However, there is a great deal of controversy over the existence of the Sangam as an academy of poets and also over the fixation of the Age of the Sangam.

The earliest work, which presents a detailed account on the three Sangams, is the commentary on *Iṛaiyanār Akapporuḷ,*

1. M. Arokiaswami, "Classical Age of the Tamils, University of Madras", 1972, p.1.

as this Akapporuḷ, Comparatively a later work is probably assigned to eight century A. D.[2] K.N. Sivaraja Pillai points out various defects and inconsistencies of the account given in the *AkapporuḷUrai,*[3] and condemns its evidence as totally unreliable, and taking into consideration of the war like-nature of the political conditions prevailed in Tamil Nadu in those days, he goes to the extent of saying, "the very idea of a literary Academy could not have been anything else than foreign."[4] He stoutly refuses to accept Akapporuḷ as a genuine work as it is so steeped into myth and mystery and thus declares the very existence of the Sangam as wholly untrue.

C. Jesudasan also rejects the idea of the existence of such a Sangam and says the term 'Sangam period' itself is a misleading one.[5] If there could have been a so-called Sangam at Madurai patronized by pāṇdiyan kings, the poets a who were very particular at immortalizing their patrons should have spoken about the Sangam also.[6] He believes that a stanza from Tirunāvukkaracar Tēvāram of the Seventh Century A.D.[7] must have been the origin of that story which could have been developed later.[8]

P.T. Srinivasa lyengar points out that no poet -who had praised the victory of a Cola monarch over the Pāṇdiya King, could have been allowed to enter into the Sangam at Madurai, patronized by Pāṇdiya kings and neither his poems could have found a place in the Sangam collections, but the facts are in reverse. Hence he comes to a conclusion that the

2. K. N. Sivaraja Pillai, "Chronology of the Early Tamils", University of Madras, 1932, p. 19.
3. Ibid. pp.24-26
4. Ibid, p.18,
5. C. Jesudasan, "History of Tamil Literature", Y.M.C.A. Publishing House, Calcutta, 1961, p.8.
6. ibid, p.9
7. Appar Tevaram, Tirupputtur Tiruttantakam, 3.
8. C. Jesudasan, Op.cit., p.8.

whole story described in Akapporuḷurai is nothing but a legend and most of the facts given in that account are irrelevant and incredible, and says, "the idea of an organised academy is a very modern one,"[9] But he himself admits that there might have been a congregation of poets of whom poet Māṅkuti Marutan was the chief,[10] and also accepts the presentation of *Tolkāppiyam* to the Royal court of Nilantaru Tiruvir Pāṇdiyan to be accepted by poets.

S. Vaiyapuri Pillai also thinks that the whole account given in the *Akapporuḷurai* is false and fabricated but at the same time confirms that there is some truth also in it,[11] because the number of the poets, 449 of the last Sangam given in *AkapporuḷUrai* more or less coṛṛesponds to the total number of poets composed the two thousand and odd poems of the Sangam literature. Further he says that Pāṇdiya kings were specially attached to Tamil than any other king of Tamil Nadu and Madurai, their capital was the centre of Tamil.[12]

P.T. Srinivasa Iyengar says that a Jaina Sangha was established to propagate the 'Triple Jewels' the main principles of Jainism at Madurai in 470 4.D., and a Buddha Sangha also was founded with a view to preaching the Buddha cult more or less in the same period. The formation of these institutions forced the saivites also to form a rival organisation to perpetuate their cult and hence arose the legend illustrated in the commentary of *Iṛaiyanār Akapporuḷ*.

S. Vaiyapuri Pillai is under the impression that the Jain and Buddha Sanghas functioned at Madurai might have served as a model for the formation of the Tamil Sangam

9. P.T. Srinivasa Iyengar, "History of the Tamils", C. Coomaraswamy Naidu & Sons, 1929, p.233.
10. Ibid., pp.238 – 239.
11. S. Vaiyapuri Pillai, "Ilakklyac Cintanaikal", p.33.
12. Cirupan. 64 - 67.

C. Jesudasan also accepts the same by his statement that the story of the Sangam arose as a counterpart of the Dramida Sangha in Madurai founded by the Jains in the fifth century A.D.[13]

This view is totally arbitrary and quite contrary to the real facts. The word 'Paṭṭi Mantapam' which occurs in *Cilappatikirām*[14] and Manimēkalai[15] itself shows clearly that the association for discussions was not unknown to the ancient Tamils.[16]

One of the main objections to accept the existence of Sangam (Tamil Academy) is that the very word Sangam is not found anywhere in Sangam literature, and hence the idea of the existence of a Sangam is nothing but an illusion. This is only misleading. The Tamil term 'avai' is the proper and most suitable equivalent to convey the idea of the Sanskrit word Sangam. This term 'avai' is used by Panampāranar, a contemporary of Tolkāppiyar, in his poetical preface to *Tolkāppiyam*, the earliest Tamil Grammar extent.[17] Other terms such as 'kūtal', 'nilaiyam', etc. also were in use and there was no necessity to adopt a Sanskrit term then. However it might have found its place in Tamil writing about the 5th century A.D. when the liberal use of Sanskrit expressions became common in Tamil Nadu. Hence the objection is purely irrelevant and need not be taken into account.

Regarding the fixation of the age of Sangam there is a general view of scholars that the total number of years assigned in the *AkapporuḷUrai*, ten thousand years must be fabulous and

13. C. Jesudasan, op.oit., p.9.
14. Cilampu. 5/102
15. Manimekalai, 1/61
16. C.E. Ramachandran, "Akananuru in its Historical setting", University of Madras, 1974, p.8.
17. Tolkappiyam, Preface, line 9.

fantastic, but to assign, one thousand years instead will be more probable.

K.R. Srinivasa lyengar observes that, "it seems to be reasonable to assume that the Sangam epoch comprised a period of about one thousand year, instead of the traditional ten thousand and we shall not be far wrong if we fix 500 B.C. and A. D. 500 as the extreme limits of the Sangam age".[18]

M. Srinivasa Iyengar, the author of Tamil studies also is of the same opinion. He says that "we shall not therefore be wrong if we look for the foundation of the first Tamil Academy or sangam somewhere between the sixth and fourth centuries before the Christian era".[19] In another place in the same work he remarks: "the first and second Academies were more or less continuous and that they existed occasionally, sometime between the fifth century B.C. and the second century A. D".[20] He further says that "there is every reason to believe that the third Academy came to an end during the second half of the sixth century".[21]

V. R. Ramachandra Dikshitar holds the same view by assigning the fifth century B.C. to the begiṉṉing of the first sangam and the fifth century A.D. to the extinction of the third sangam.[22]

N. Subrahmanian concludes that the Sangam age is the period of a few centuries immediately preceding or succeeding the Christian era.[23]

18. R.C. Majumdar, "History and Culture of the Indian people", Vol. II, Bharatiya Vidya Bhavan Series, p. 293.
19. M. Srinivasa Iyengar, "Tamil Studies", The Guardian Press, Madras, p. 235.
20. Ibid., p. 244.
21. Ibid., p. 250.
22. V.R. Ramachandra Dikshitar, "Studies in Tamil Literature and History", University of Madras, 1936. P.21.
23. N. Subrahmanian, "Sangam Polity", Ennes Pubs., Madurai, p. 26.

P.T. Srinivasa Iyengar categorically accepts the antiquity of the Tamil Literature, He says that the earliest Tamil poems now clearly to represent the later stage of literary development, as the language is highly refined and composed in strict metrical system with complicated conventions. He observes that "possibly the earliest songs were in the unrefined dialects, actually spoken; but they have all died just as have perished the early Sanskrit ballads".[24]

V. Kanagasabai Pillai points out that, "the Augustan period of Tamil literature was, I should say, in the first century of the Christian era, and the last college of poets was then held in Madurai in the court of the Tamil King Ugra Pāṇdya."[25] Thus he accepts that the third Sangam flourished in the first century A.D. and the Tamil literature was highly developed then.

K.A. Nilakanta Sastri says that "we are therefore bound to assume, until much stronger proof to the contrary is forthcoming than has been put forward so far, that the Sangam age lies in the early centuries of the Christian era."[26]

V.A. Smith also expresses the same idea in his Early History of India. The scholars who maintain the early date of the best Tamil poems are right and the Augustan age of Tamil Literature may be placed in the first three centuries of the Christian era.[27]

N. Subrahmaniam writes, in his History of Tamilnad (p.46) that, "the age of the Sangam could be taken to be a period of six centuries, from the 3rd century B.C. to the 3rd century A.D."

24. P.T. Srinivasa Iyengar, "History of the Tamils", p. 149.
25. V. Kanagasabai Pillai, "The Tamils Eighteen Hundred Years Ago", Kazhagam, 1966, p. 3.
26. K.A. Nilakanta Sastri, "The Pandyan Kingdom", Luzac & Co., London, 1929, p. 24.
27. V.A. Smith, "Early History of India", p. 445.

In the light of the above views, we can safely assume that the Sangam age should have been spread over a number of centuries around the Christian era, and the earliest date could be assigned in 500 B.C. and Tamil was a well developed language even at 500 B.C.

The short Tamil inscriptions found in the caverns in hills chiselled in Brahmi script created doubts among the scholars about the well developed stage of Tamil by 500 B.C.

K.A. Nilakanta Sastri observes that, "though the script of these inscriptions is Brahmi of the southern variety their language is seen to be Tamil still in its formative stages.[28] But he himself admits that these inscriptions from the caverns have not fully elucidated.[29] Further these inscriptions contain only the names of either the donor or the dweller of the cavern and the cavern too was donated by Jaina or Buddhists of Northern India, who were alien to Tamil, and hence Brahmi script was used.

C.E. Ramachandran clearly points out that "it is not fair to think that Tamil was not a well developed language by 500 B.C."[30]

T.V. Sadaiva Pandaraṭṭar considering the synchronism of Cēran Cenkuṭṭuvan, who celebrated the erection of Kaṇṇagi statue at his capital, and Gajabahu I, King of Ceylon, who attended the above celebration and the total absence of reference in Sangam literature to the Pallavas, who gained prominence during the later half of the third century A.D., concludes that the third Sangam might have ended during the first half of the third century A.D.[31]

28. K.A. Nilakanta Sastri, "Comprehensive History of India", Vol. II, p. 501.
29. Ibid., p. 500.
30. C.E. Ramachandran, "Op.cit"., p. 5.
31. T.V. Sadasiva Pandarattar, "A. History of Tamil Literature (250 – 600 A.D.)", pp. 1 – 4.

T.P. Meenakshisundaram Pillai taking into account the Greek and Roman trade with Tamils mentioned in Sangam literature and the excavation at Arikāmēdu near Pondicheṛṛy observes that "As the Roman trade with the East, more or less ceased by the third century, this Sangam literature may be assigned to the first three centuries of the Christian era."[32]

C.E. Ramachandran accepting the above view says that "the extant Tamil classics according to the commentary on Iṛaiyanār Akapporuḷ belonged to the third Sangam. The period of the third Sangam can be roughly taken to the first three centuries of the Christian era."[33]

Therefore it may not be wrong to assign the first three centuries of the Christian era to the third Sangam, and the Sangam literature one of which is Paṭṭinappālai.

Paṭṭinappālai

The title of this poem is Paṭṭinappālai, which consists of two separate terms namely 'Paṭṭinam' and 'Pālai'. 'Paṭṭinam' is the name of a place viz., Kāvirippūmpaṭṭinam, and 'Pālai' is the name given to a particular region of land (desert region) as well as a particular behaviour (Separation of lovers) of the people (Tamils) described by Tamil Grammar.

Paṭṭinam

The term 'Paṭṭinam'is a common name given either to a village or a town on the sea-shore. For example, Kayal Paṭṭinam, Kulasēkaran Paṭṭinam, Cāluvaṇaicken Paṭṭinam, Atirāmapaṭṭinam, Nāgappaṭṭinam, Kavērippaṭṭinam (Kāviripūmpaṭṭinam,Ciatrirank appaṭṭinam (Sadrās) etc. on the Cora mandal coast may be men-

32. T.P. Meeaakahisundaram Pillai, "A History of Tamil Literature", p.17.
33. C.E. Ramachandran, "Op.cit"., p.5.

tioned. But in this context Paṭṭinam stands for Kāvirippūmpaṭṭinam[34] which was the capital and main sea port of the mighty cholas of the Sangam age.

Sangam classics mentioned Kāvirippumpaṭṭinam as Pukār[35] and Pūmpukār.[36] Pukār means in general a river-mouth that is the place where a river flows into the sea. But here it means the city situated on the banks of ancient and sacred river kāviri at its mouth that is Kāvirippūmpaṭṭinam.[37] This Pukār is also mentioned as Pumpukār[38] which means the beautiful Pukār.

Cilappatikārram mentions this city as 'Kāvirippaṭappaippaṭṭinam'[39] whereas Manimēkalai mentions this city as 'Kāvirip paṭappai naṇṇakar'[40] which means Kāvirippūmpaṭṭinam with full of groves on either side of Kāviri at its mouth. 'Nagar' means either a town or a city that is Kāvirippūmpaṭṭinam, *Manimekalai* mentions this city as 'kākanti'[41] also, because it was governed by a chieftain named Kakantan.

It is clear that the term Paṭṭinam stands for Kāvirippūmpaṭṭinam, and now we shall take the other term Pālai.

Pālai

The term 'Pālai' as it is used in this title is one of the five main divisions of Akaṭṭiṇai, described in *Tolkāppiyam*, the earliest Tamil Grammar extant.

34. Pattina. 218
35. Ibid. 173
36. Cilambu. I. 1. 10.
37. Pattina. 173.
38. Cilambu. I. 1. 10.
39. Ibid. 15/151.
40. Manimekalai 25/16
41. Ibid. 22/37

To understand the term 'Pālai' in its real sense, it will be beṭṭer to trace the fundamentals of this particular section of the Tamil Grammar 'Poruḷ'.

'Poruḷ' the third part of the Tamil Grammar is divided into two broad divisions called Akam (Akaṭṭiṇai or Akapporuḷ) and Puram (Puṛaṭṭiṇai or Purapporuḷ), Akam denotes inner or things concerned with love, whereas Puram denotes everything pertaining to worldly life except things concerned with love.

The ancient Tamils noted that the habitable parts of the land might be divided into five natural regions and gave a common name to them 'tiṇai'. The regions or tiṇai were called Kuṛinci (hilly region), Mullai (forest regions), Marutam (agricultural region), Neytal (Coastal region) and Pālai (desert region). Among these five regions, the first four regions are of permanent nature and the fifth region cannot be considered to be so. Because the Mullai and Kuṛinci regions, by nature's blessings are of interchangeable into Pālai region and vice versa.[42]

They also observed that the manifestation of human life coṛṛesponds to the characteristics of the environment in which each tribe grown. Hence the term tiṇai was also used in the sense of behaviour. The behaviour of Pālai is said to be the separation of lovers. According to the Tamil Grammarians, separation may take place due to learning, earning wealth of defending the country.

The central idea or the theme of the poem is the separation of lovers, due to the departure of the hero in search of fortune, so that they can lead a happy married life. It is notable that the behaviour - separation, 'Pālai' is attributed

42. Cilampu. 11/64 – 66

to the region 'Pālai. Hence the term 'Pālai' with reference to the title is the separation of lovers. However the net result is a total refusal of the hero to leave his mate and go in search of wealth, even though he could get the wealthy 'Paṭṭinam' itself,[43] and determines to stay with his love. Because the way (Pālai or desert) through which he has to go is more horrible than the horror caused by the spear of Tirumāvaḷavan aimed at his enemies. But at the same time the pleasure he gets by being with his love is more pleasant that the virtuous reign of the same Tirumāvaḷavan. The Paṭṭinam which is compared with wealth is graphically described in the first part of the poem,[44] and the dangers of the 'Pālai' the track through which he has to go is given comparatively to the destruction caused to his enemies by Tirumāvaḷavan .[45]

Author

The author of this poem is Kaṭiyalūr Uruṭṭiran Kaṇṇanar. Kaṇṇan is his personal name and the suffix 'ār' is an honorific term denoting respect given to him as a poet, 'Uruthiran' is the name of his father added before his name in order to differentiate him from other persons with the same name. Nowadays we use the first leṭṭer of the father's name of a person as his initial, but in those days instead of using initials, the name was written in full. In the same way, Kaṭiyalūr the name of his birth place also was written before the name of his father Uruṭṭiran, Hence his full name was Kaṭiyalūr Uruṭṭiran Kaṇṇanar.

It is impossible to ascertain where is or was Kaṭiyalūr. However M. Rajamanickam puts forth a probable suggestion that this Kaṭiyalūr may be identified with the pre-

43. Pattina. 218 – 220.
44. Ibid. 218.
45. Ibid. 228 - 282

sent 'Kaṭukkaḷur', a hamlet some seven miles south west of Ceyyūr, a prominent place in Maturantakam Taluk of Chinglepet District.[46]

The central idea or the theme of the poem is the separation of lovers due to the departure of the hero, in search of fortune, so that they can lead a happy married life. This kind of separation of lovers is called 'Pālai', one of the five main divisions of Akaṭṭiṇai in Tamil Grammar.

Perumpāṇāṟṟuppaṭai, one of the same groups of *Paṭṭuppāṭṭu* or the Ten idylls is also said to be his composition but the theme is completely a different one and belongs to Puṟaṭṭiṇai.

One verse in *Akanāṉūru* (167) and one verse in *Kuruntokai* (352) are also said to be his compositions and the theme of these two verses also are of 'Pālait-tiṇai'.

It is from his verses evidently clear that he was quite acquainted with those people about whom he speaks and the places about those he describes. For instance, he literally describes the day-today life of the veḷaḷar (agriculturist), vaṇikar (merchant) and mīnavar (fishermen). In the same ways he presents a complete and vivid pen picture of Kāvirippūmpaṭṭinam, the then Cola port which caṟṟied extensive trade and commerce, and the duties of the excise officials are given in detail. Paṭṭinappālai can be taken as an authentic source of history of trade and commerce of the Tamils during the Sangam age.

46. M. Rajamanickam, "A Critical Study in Pattuppattu", p.72.

Patron

Tirumāvaḷavan, as per the text, is the patron of *Paṭṭinappālai.* It speaks about his early heroic deeds in detail.[47] Though it speaks about wars and victories in detail to some extent, it leaves us in darkness, as there is no mention of either the names of the kings who had suffered defeat at his hands or the places captured by him.[48] It reveals that he had enriched his kingdom by creating villages out of forest and deepening the tanks etc., and won the goodwill of his subjects. We, at the end of the poem, hear about his children and consorts as well. These are the only things that we can gather about his personal history from the text.

However Ilanko Atikal, author of Cilappatikāram provides some more information about Tirumāvaḷavan. It says that Tirumāvaḷavan , in order to get foes to fight at least in the north went up to Himalayas. On his returning the kings of vacciratēca, Makatatēca and Avantitēca presented the Cola monarch with 'Koṟṟappantar', 'Paṭṭimaṇṭapam' and 'tōraṇavāyil' respectively. It seems that no other Sangam classics speak about Tirumāvaḷavan. Therefore let us examine the facts provided by them.

Paṭṭinappālai reveals that Tirumāvaḷavan gained his victories over the kings in South, West and North of his kingdom; but *Cilappatikāram* describes his expedition to north, upto Himalayas; without any resistance but the obstruction of Himalayas. So he imprinted his Royal emblem – the tiger mark on it and returned. Thus these two works do not agree in any manner. Apart from this the omission of the expedition to Himalayas in *Paṭṭinappālai* is unacceptable as it must be a great achievement in those days. No doubt

47. Pattina. 220 – 227.
48. Ibid. 274 – 282.

Uruṭṭiran Kaṇṇanar cannot go wrong as he was a contemporary of Tirumāvaḷavan , and hence there is no other alternative but to allow some margin to the version of Iḷankō Aṭikaḷ.

It is said that Tirumāvaḷavan is none other than Karikālan, a great Cola monarch who had won the battles at veṇṇi[49] and Vakaipparantalai.[50] Aṭiyārkkunallār in his celebrated commentary to Cilappatikāram identifies this Tirumāvaḷavan with Karikālan.[51] But he seems to be unaware of the fact that the name of Karikālan is mentioned twice in two different places in the same work by the same author.[52] If Tirumāvaḷavan is none other than Karikālan, Iḷankō Aṭikaḷ could not have mentioned the same king with two different names in three different places. Hence it is clear that Iḷankō Aṭikaḷ did not consider the two Cola kings as one and the same king.

It is noteworthy that the expedition to Himalayas by Tirumāvaḷavan is mentioned in no other work. So it may be supposed that Iḷankō Aṭikaḷ might have said this only for the sake of formality, because he had to give this credit later to Imayavarampan Netuncēralātan, the Cēra king.

Ceyankontar, the author of the well known Kalinkaṭṭupparani speaks about the expedition of Karikālan to Himalayas,[53] but it has no mention in any of the Sangam classics, which glorify him with his great victories over the Cēra, Pāṇdiya kings and eleven velir (minor kings) at Veṇṇi and Vakaipparantalai as we have seen already. Hence this too seems to be unreliable. It is also notable that a separate book written on Tirumāvaḷavan which identifies him with Karikālan by Pulavar K. Govindan, the author of the Kings

49. Akam 246; porunar. 146 – 148.
50. Ibid. 125
51. Cilampu. 5/90
52. Ibid. 6/159; 21/11
53. Kalinkattup parani, verse 196.

and the Poets of the Sangam age, keeps silence on this expedition.

There are references in Sangam classics about three other Cola kings with similar name with slight differences. Purananuru speaks about (Colan Kuraappallit tunoiya) PerunTirumāvaḷavan ,[54] Netumavalavan alias Colan Kulamuṟṟattu tunciya killi valavan[55] and Mavalattan the younger brother of Colan Nalankilli.[56] These names themselves show clearly that these kings were different from Tirumāvaḷavan of *Paṭṭinappālai.*

Porunar Aṟṟuppatai, one of the Ten Idylls, was composed in praise of karikal valavan,[57] by Mutaṭṭamak kaṉṉiyar and in the same way Paṭṭinappālai, another idyll of the same group, was composed in praise of Tirumāvaḷavan [58] by Uruṭṭiran Kaṇṇanar. But, somehow or other the scholars believed that Karikal Valavan and Tirumavalavan were one and the same king.

Aṭiyārkkunallār in his commentary identified Tirumāvaḷavan with Karikālan.[59] Naccinarkkiniyar, equally celebrated commentator of Sangam classics, faithfully followed him[60] and it was universally accepted. But some three dēcades ago some renowned scholars raised objection to this traditional view.

Some of the reasons for their objections were:

54 Puram. 58
55. Ibid. 228
56. Ibid. 43
57. Porunar. 148
58. Pattina. 299
59. Cilambu. 5/90
60. Pattina. 299

Porunar Aṛṛuppatai mentions karikal valavan as the patron[61] but Paṭṭinappālai mentions Tirumāvaḷavan as the patron.[62] Hence these two kings with different names cannot be one and the same king.

Porunar Aṛṛuppatai describes the battle of Veṇṇi won by Karikal valavan[63] but there is no mention about this in Paṭṭinappālai.

Porunar Aṛṛuppatai mentions no other battle than Veṇṇi, but *Paṭṭinappālai* provides a series of military exploits of Tirumāvaḷavan .

Porunar Aṛṛuppatai reveals that Karikal Valavan got his right when he was in his mother's womb[64] and ruled his kingdom from his very childhood[65] but Paṭṭinappālai reveals that Tirumāvaḷavan was in the prison cell in his childhood, and in course of time he got back his kingdom by defeating his enemies.[66] These are contrary to one another

The answers given for these are:

Porunar Aṛṛuppatai mentions Karikal Valavan,[67] and *Paṭṭinappālai* mentions Tiruniavalavan.[68] The same *Porunar Aṛṛuppatai* reveals that Uruvappakrer Ilanchetceṇṇi, was the father of Karikal Valavan.[69] Poet Paranar was a contemporary to Uruvappakrer Ilancetceṇṇi and he had praised Ilancetceṇṇi in a poem.[70] The same Paranar mentions Kari-

61. Porunar. 148
62. Pattina 299
63. Porunar. 147
64. Ibid. 132.
65. Ibid. 137 – 138.
66. Ibid. 220 – 227.
67. Ibid. 148.
68. Pattina. 299.
69. Porunar. 130.
70. Puram, 4.

kal Valavan as 'Peruvalak Karikal'.[71] The terms 'Peruvalan' and 'mavalan' are the same. Hence there is no difference between the two names, Karikal Valavan and Tirumāvaḷavan .

No doubt there is no reference to the battle of Veṇṇi in *Paṭṭinappālai* but no one can compel a poet to include anything in his poem.

Porunar Aṛṛuppatai might have been composed soon after his victory at the battle of Veṇṇi. Hence there is no mention about his later victories.

The contents of the passage describes the childhood of Karikal Valavan in *Porunar Aṛṛuppatai*[72] and the contents of the passage explaining the childhood activities of Tirumāvaḷavan in *Paṭṭinappālai*[73] are the same. The matter mentioned in line 132 of *Porunar Aṛṛuppatai* is given in line 227 of Paṭṭinappālai. Further the note about the victories of Karikal Valavan over his enemies given in line 133 of *Porunar Aṛṛuppatai,* is given in detail in the passage of *Paṭṭinappālai.*[74] Hence there is no difference between the contents of the said two passages.

However the answers given to the objections do not seem to be either appropriate or acceptable. Hence there is no possibility of identifying Tirumāvaḷavan with Karikal Valavan.

The Place of Paṭṭinappālai in the Sangam Literature

The Sangam literature consists of the *Paṭṭuppāṭṭu* (the Ten Idylls), the *Eṭṭuṭṭokai* (the Eight Anthologies) and the *Patinenkilkanakku* (Eighteen Minor works). Nowadays the twin

71. Akam, 175/18.
72. Porunar. 132 – 138.
73. Pattina. 220 – 227.
74. Ibid. 220 – 227.

epics *Cilappatikāram* and *Manimēkalai* also are considered to be Sangam literature. The term *Patinenkil kanakku* implies that there might have been one such collection called *Patinen Merkanakku* (Eighteen Major works). Probably consisting of *Paṭṭuppāṭṭu* and *Eṭṭuṭṭokai*, totaly eighteen works. In this context the term 'kanakku' means a book.[75]

The primitive man lived next to nature, loved it and believed it to be his lord and God and was interested only in nature and sang all about nature; later he felt himself a member of the society to which he had to oblige and then the two main aspects of human life, love and war, also found place in his songs, and classical Tamil works are a striking Illustration to these things. They also serve as a valuable source of history of Tamil Nadu.

The subject matter of Sangam literature is divided into two broad divisions namely Akam and Puram and they are called Akaṭṭiṇai and Puṛaṭṭiṇai. Akam speaks everything about love whereas Puram deals with all other worldly affairs such as war, government, society, etc. Akam treats of love themes and they are classified into five main sections viz, Mullai (patience of a wife who is separated from her husband and her deep longing for his, return), Kurinci (pre maritial love), Marutam (married life and its consequences), Neytal (lamentations of a separated wife) and Pālai (separation of lovers). Puram also is classified into five sections and they are vetci, vanci, uliṇai, tumpai and vakai. According to Tamil literary convention a poet should not mention the names of lovers, but he was free to introduce his patron directly describing his achievements etc., and such patron was called 'Paṭṭutait talaivan.'

75. Naltiyar, Avaiyarital 4; Palamoli 61.

Among the Sangam classics the verses of Paṭṭuppāṭṭu deserve most prominent mention as each of them are considered to be separate and complete works and they are richly descriptive and well finished.

P. Sundaram Pillai aptly observes: "They are charming portraits of nature in some of her pleasant and striking moods and for soberness of thought and accuracy of representation, they will bear comparison with anything in the whole realm of literature."[76]

Paṭṭuppāṭṭu verses are composed in aciriyam or akavarpa,[77] which has three lines as minimum and thousand lines as maximum limit.[78] Composition of Akavarpa which has four metrical foot (cir) in each line is very simple. If an akavarpa line is short of four metrical foot, either with two or three metrical foot, it will be called 'vancippa'. *Paṭṭinappālai* which has 301 lines is largely mixed vancippa lines and hence it is also called 'vanci netumpaṭṭu'

The descriptive pen-pictures of the ancient Tamil poets indicate their first hand acquaintance with Nature and it is true that they confined themselves only to concrete conceptions and paid no attention to any kind of abstract ideas. An idyll, as a short story, is a descriptive poem of some picturesque scene or incident. Among the Ten idylls, five belongs to Aṟṟuppatai. An Aṟṟuppatai is a poem which a bard who had received gifts from his patron either a king or a chieftain - directs another bard and his group to the same patron, so as to enable him to receive rich gifts. They are: *Tirumurukaṟṟuppatai* containing 317 lines, composed by Nakkirar, is a devotional song on Lord Murugan. *Porunar Aṟṟuppatai,* with 248 lines praising the famous Cola king

76. Pattuppattu, Translated by J.Y. Chelliah, Kazhagam, 1962, p.xv.
77. Tol. Porul. 393.
78. Ibid. 469.

Karikal Valavan was composed by Mutaṭṭamak Kaṇṇiyar. Cirupanaṟṟuppatai with 269 lines, praising Nalliyak kotan, a chieftain under the Cola king, was composed by Nallur Naṭṭaṭṭanar, *Perumpāṇāṟṟuppaṭai* with 500 lines, was composed by Kaṭiyalūr Uruṭṭiran Kaṇṇanar in praise of Tontaiman Ilanthiraiyan. *Malaipatukatam* with 583 lines, the second longest among the Ten Idylls is composed on the lines of Aṟṟuppatai. In this poem a bard who received gifts from Nanaan directs a dancer and his group to the same patron for the purpose of receiving gifts, and hence it is also called Kuṭṭar aṟṟuppatai (kuṭṭar - dancer). The author Perunkaucikanar compares a mountain and the various sounds heard there to a male elephant and its secretion and thus got the title *Malaipatukatam*.

Mullaippaṭṭu with 103 lines, the shortest among the verses of *Paṭṭuppāṭṭu*, is based on the subjective element of Mullaiṭṭiṇai. It speaks about the mental condition of a separated wife from her husband who was away in the battlefield. The composer is Napputanar.

Kuṟincippaṭṭu with 262 lines is based on the subjective element of Kuṟincit tiṇai that is pre-marital love or love at first sight. This contains a fine description of mountain scenery and speaks about as many as ninety nine flowers including Kuṟinci flower which will blossom once in twelve years and they are found largely on the Western Ghats especially on the Nilgiris. This was composed by Kapilar in order to impart Tamil knowledge to Prakaṭṭan, an Aryan king.

Netunalvadai with 188 lines, composed by Nakkirar is based on the subjective element of Mullait tiṇai, which belongs to Akam. But it contains an indirect reference to Pāṇdiyan king who was away in the war front and hence it is considered to be of vakait tiṇai, which is a part of Puṟaṭṭiṇai, as the hero of the poem should not be mentioned anyway in a poem which belongs to Akaṭṭiṇai.

Paṭṭinappālai with 301 lines, a fairly long verse, has a fine pen-picture of Kāvirippūmpaṭṭinam and its suburbs, which was the then Cola capital and the main sea-port; it also gives a detailed account of the destruction caused by Tirumāvaḷavan, the paṭṭutai talaivan to his enemy's countries. It is based on the subjective element of Pālaiṭṭiṇai which is a part of Akaṭṭiṇai and the author is Kaṭiyalūr Uruṭṭiran Kaṇṇanar.

Maturaikkanci with 782 lines, the longest among the ten idylls is based on the subjective element of Kanciṭṭiṇai, which belongs to Puram. Kailclṭṭiṇai indicates the mortality of human beings. The author Mankuti Marutan by way of praising the Pandiyan king Netunceliyan presents a detailed description of his kingdom, his administration and his capital Madurai.

According to Tamil literary convention, *Paṭṭinappālai* is single verse with 301 lines can be defined as an epic. This is a special feature of *Paṭṭinappālai*. The convention prescribes that an epic should be adorned by an incomparable hero and his masterly achievement. Besides this there should be pen-pictures describing the country, the city, the suburbs, the river, the sea, etc. There is ample scope for these things in Paṭṭinappālai.

Tirumāvaḷavan , the hero and his achievement are vivdly illustrated in the poem. The river Kāviri is graphically described in a nut-shell. There are excellent pen pictures describing the village scenery, the activities including the sports and pastime of the village rustics, as well as the most civilized citizens. The busy customs house with the loyal and dutiful tariff collections, flags flying at various places in the city besides colourful flags stop the masts of ships anchored at the sea-port, spacious mansions showing the skilful art and architecture of those days with shining paintings, the demon guarded temple as well as the pallis of Jains and Buddhists, the scenery at the mouth of the River Kāviri and all other such things which formparts of an epic. Now we can see a few of them.

Tirumāvaḷavan , a great Cola king of the Sangam age, is the incomparable hero (paṭṭutait talaivan) of Paṭṭinappālai.

The Young prince, as a tiger cub had grown in a cage, had grown and gained strength when he was in the enemy's prison and as a tusker escaped from the deep pit, escaped by his calculated plans and valour; and regained his kingdom.

Tirumāvaḷavan longed for more territory by victory and marched on with his huge tuskers followed by cavalries and soldiers and his thundering war drums frightened the foes. The tuskers destroyed the ramparts, broke open the strong gates and trampled down the crowned heads of enemy kings. The valiant foes either fell at his feet, or were completely destroyed.

Oliyar chiefs surrendered themselves and the ancient Aruvalar kings offered their services while the Goorg king grew pale and fainted; the Pāṇdiya king who roused his anger was scared. The minor Shepherd kings and the Irunkovel kings were routed. In short, he possessed a great amount of strength to overthrow his enemy kings with valiant troops of power and zeal, and wherever he marched on he was crowned with success. Such was the greatness of Tirumāvaḷavan, the immortal hero (Paṭṭutait talaivan) of *Paṭṭinappālai.*

The ancient and sacred river kāviri, even at the times of severe drought due to uṭṭer failure of rain, makes the vast

Cola country fertile and ever green by its overflowing water mingled with mineral wealth and thus the Cola country became the 'Gift of Kāviri' and is praised as the 'Granary of south India'.

Wherever we look we see nothing but the green paddy fields and the sweet sugarcane gardens. Besides, there are fertile groves of coconut trees, plantain trees, arēca palms, and the palmyra trees all with bunches and the sweet mango trees. There are turmeric plants, rooty Indian kales plants and medicinal ginger plants.

Beautiful maids who are watching the drying grains scare away the fowls by throwing there costly golden ear-rings. The three wheeled toy chariots pulled by children are obstructed by those jewels thrown by the maids.

There are alms houses with tiger marked strong doors and the massive wall painted with the figure of Tirumakal, wherefrom the water decanted from cooked rice flows through the street like a river.

The hermits with matted locks perform their daily sacrifices and the cuckoos live nearby shun the smoke from the oblations fire; fly away with their black mates and stay in the demon guarded kali temple where the pebble-swallowing doves live.

Large ponds with the lofty temple on the bund appear like the full moon amidst the asterism Makam and the twin lakes which can afford such lust as felt in this birth as well as in the next are also on the sea-shore of the city.

As the ever bright planets move amidst the glittering stars, the strong men amidst the gathered common folk fight with hands and weapons on the wrestling ground arid the stones fly from their slings scare away the birds on the age old palmyra trees.

There are flags flying at the entrance of the temples to be worshipped by the passers by. There are banners fixed on the curved bars over the locked baskets of various kinds of tasty victuals. Great scholars have hoisted flags inviting scholars who can make disputation with them. Beautiful flags of various countries are flying atop the masts of the ships anchored at the port of Pukār. There are flags flying at the gates of toddy shops also, as a sign to mark the sale. The shadows of all these flags prevent the sun's rays from entering the city streets.

Considering all these things it can be justified that Paṭṭinappālai is an epic.

Kaṭiyalūr Uruṭṭiran Kaṇṇanar has clearly exhibited his masterly art of literary theme by combining the subjective elements of both akam and puram in one and the same poem, Paṭṭinappālai. This is another special feature of Paṭṭinappālai.

There are five main divisions of Puram which are considered to be parallel to the five main divisions of Akam. According to this grammatical convention Vakait tiṇai of Puram is parallel to Pālaiṭṭiṇai of Akam.[79] The subjective element of Pālai is separation of lovers while the subjective element of Vakai is to gain victory over the enemy. Hence the subjective elements of Pālai and Vakai are completely different from one another. However the author has wonderfully brought them together without causing any change in the original aspects of their subjective elements.

In this context Pālai also is made into a victory as the separating itself has not taken place. The mind prompted the hero (Kilavit talaivan) to leave his consort and go in search of a fortune, but he totally refused to go and stayed with his charming mate. Thus he won the battle with his mind and became vic-

79. Tol. Porul. 73

torious, while Tirumāvaḷavan (Paṭṭutait talaivan) won the war with his enemy kings and became victorious. Thus the author has well proved the parallelism of both vakai and Pālai, and this poem is considered to be the-best literary example for the said grammatical convention. Hence Paṭṭinappālai has an important place among the Sangam literature.

Paṭṭinappālai as a Source of History

The history of Tamil Nadu may cover more than twenty five centuries consisting of the Ancient, Medieval and Modern periods, but our concern is only with the ancient or the Sangam period. The history of the past of any country can be written only on the basis of the relevant and reliable sources available. The sources may be grouped into epigraphical data, numismatics, archaeology and literature.

Among these sources the epigraphical data, which can be more useful is very limited and that too is not within the limits of Tamil Nadu.

The earliest inscriptions in Tamil Nadu are the short inscriptions found in the natural waves which contain either the names of the carvers of the rock-bed, or the occupants and so are of no use for/the purpose. Hence Dr. Subrahmanian observes, "that source does not yield much material for a study of the history of the Sangam age for we have practically no contemporary local epigraphical evidence to coṛṛoborate the information obtained from other sources."[80]

The Velvikkuti Grant of Parantaka Netuncataiyan (795-815) reveals the renewal of the grant by the Pāṇḍiyan Palyakacalai Mutukutumi Peruvaluti of the Sangam age. A similar reference about the Panidiyan Netunceliyan of Talai-

80. N. Subrahmanian, Sangam Polity, Ennes Publications, Madurai, p.15.

yalankanam fame is given in larger Siṇṇamanur Plates. The inscriptions at Kutumiyamalai and at Tirukkovalur also are of very useful for the purpose.[81]

Numismatics evidence also is very limited, as the coins contain neither the date nor the king to whom they belong. They belong either to Pāṇdiyas or to Colas of that age. Large numbers of Roman coins are found at Arikkametu and near Madurai only ascertain the trade with Roman and other foreigners.

Archaeology is very useful for it confirms the information given by literature, and helps us to fix the Sangam age, and to assign the conditions and events of that period.

Literature concerning to our purpose, is the most useful and reliable source of history. This can be divided into three groups namely foreign, Sanskrit and Sangam literature.

Among the foreign writers Megasthenes, Strabo, Pliny and Ptolemy of the west, and Pan Kou, Fahien, Hiuen Tsang of the East are prominent and their accounts besides periplus and Peutingerian Tables are very useful.

Sanskrit literatures are not much useful as they simply mention the name of either a king or a place or any valuable material such as pearl, etc.

The whole of Sangam literature, *Paṭṭuppāṭṭu, Eṭṭut tokai, Patinenkilkanakku,* the twin epics as well as the remnant parts of Takatur Yaṭṭirai and *Peruntevanar Bharatam* are of most useful for the purpose.

But K.A. Nilakanata Sastri says, "while literature is in other countries the bedrock of history, in India it is of-

81. Ibid., p. 17.

ten a snare."[82] Dr. C.E. Ramachandran observes, "Generally speaking this is not far from the truth but a careful study and dispassionate shifting of relevant material from the miscellaneous heap is bound to yield valuable grains of historical information which, if properly used can form the basis of correct historical evaluations.[83] Hence N. Subrahmaniam concludes that "there can be no doubt that the historical data contained in these works clearly relate to a compact and well defined period in the histroy of Tamilakam and it will not be wrong to call that period the Sangam period"[84]

Sangam literature may be considered as the more valuable and most reliable source of history of Tamil Nadu of that period that the literature of any other period as the Sangam poets were not inhibited by excessively religious or did actic or any other extraneous sentiments. The verses of Sangam poets belong to a spontaneous and natural type of poetry which is free from gross exaggeration and uṇṇatural hyperbole, and by the simplicity and directness, of smiles they serve as a useful and dependable source of history of Tamilnadu.

It may be quite natural to presume that the poems belong to puram will provide with complete information to history of that period and Patiṟṟuppaṭṭu and Purananuru of the Sangam literature are the best example. But at the same time it will not be wrong to conclude that no historical data can be obtained from verses belonging to Akam. They also incidentally give valuable information that too in an indirect way.

For instance, we hear about the Velan Veriyatal[85] and the generous chieftain Ori[86] in *Naṟṟiṇai*, the minor kings

82. K.A. Nilakanta Sastri, The Cholas, Vol.1, University of Madras, 1935, p. 16.
83. C.E. Ramachandran, Op.cit., p.8.
84. N. Subrahmanian, Op.cit., p.22.
85. Narrinai, 134.
86. Ibid, 152.

Akutai[87] and Naṇṇan[88] in *Kuruntokai*; the battles of Veṇṇi[89] and Vakaipparantalai[90] in *Akanānūru* and so on.

Naṟṟiṇai, Kuruntokai and *Akanānūru* which exclusively speak about Akam (love) are also full of references to historical personages and events.

Paṭṭinappālai is a best source book of history of Tamil Nadu during the early centuries of the Christian era. Paṭṭinappālai contains many references about the political, social, economical and religious conditions of Tamil Nadu of those days.

It speaks about Tirumāvaḷavan the Cola king of the Sangam age,[91] his imprisonment and escape,[92] conquests over Oliyar,[93] Aruvalar,[94] Kutakar,[95] Pandiyan,[96] Potuvan[97] and Irunkovel,[98] and presents a fine pen-picture of his mighty wars and battlefields.[99] However Paṭṭinappālai provides a greater with of information relating to social, economical, religious and cultural aspects of history.

We see the nearby hamlets to one another in the vast Cola country,[100] the spacious courtyards in front of the houses,[101] the young maids who are watching the drying grains scare away the fowls by throwing their golden earrings,[102] the three

87. Kuru, 298.
88. Ibid, 292
89. Akam, 246
90. Ibid, 55.
91. Pattina, 299
92. Ibid., 220 – 227
93. Ibid., 274
94. Ibid., 275
95. Ibid., 276
96. Ibid., 277
97. Ibid., 281
98. Ibid., 282
99. Ibid., 226/237
100. Ibid., 28
101. Ibid., 20
102. Ibid., 20 – 23

wheeled toy chariots pulled by children are obstructed by those earrings,[103] the large gathering at the wrestling ground where the valiant men fight with hands to hands and weapons and the stones fly from their stings scare away the birds on the tall palmyra trees,[104] the fishermen on the full moon day neglecting their work, stay with their mates, clad in garments of green leaves eat and play all day long,[105] the people to cleanse their sins take bath in the rearing sea at the junction of Kāviri and then bathe in the fresh water to wash the salt[106] and the people enjoying the music and drama during the night time,[107] The veḷaḷars cultivated their lands and helped the Brahmins to do their duties and sacrifices.[108] The citizens were kind and hospitable to the foreigners[109] and the captured women were entrusted with the temple duties such as lighting etc.

Paṭṭinappālai presents besides fertile paddy fields arid sweet sugarcane groves, the backbone of the country's economy then,[110] an evergreen botanical garden of medicinal ginger plants, turmeric plants, rooty Indian kales plants, plantain trees, mango trees, areca palls, coconut trees and palmyra trees all with full of bunches which also supplemented the country's economy.[111] The paddy was given in barter to salt.[112] The working of the customs house, and its officials who carefully collect the import and export duties which helped the royal exchequer to a great extent and stamp the tiger mark, the royal emblem on the tax collected bags

103. Ibid.,
104. Ibid., 69 – 74
105. Ibid., 90 – 96
106. Ibid., 97 – 100
107. Ibid., 113
108. Ibid., 199 – 205
109. Ibid., 216 – 217
110. Ibid., 8 – 9
111. Ibid., 16 – 19
112. Ibid., 29 – 30

and a list of goods and the places wherefrom they came and all such things are vividly given in a nutshell.[113]

The tiger figure on the doors and the Tirumakal figures on the walls of the alms house[114] and various kinds of pictures on the palace walls are all beautifully painted with shining colours.

There are big houses with spacious courtyards in the hamlets.[115] There in the capital city are cloud capped, storied buildings with large and small halls, provided with windows and doors both large and small with spacious cloisters and the pials around the building which can be reached by ladders with close-set rungs.[116]

There are references about the Jains and Buddhist pallis,[117] Kali temples,[118] 'kantu' (God's emblem),[119] hermits and sacrifices,[120] and the festival of Gevvel 'Murugan)[121] which all can reveal the religious conditions of those days.

The ladies wore silk and coṭṭon dresses [122] and drank wine.[123] The garland worn by men were called 'kaṇṇi' and the garland worn by ladies were called 'kotai' by which the women are called 'kotai' and such was their civilisation even before twenty centuries ago.

In this way, *Paṭṭinappālai* can afford many more historical facts and this is the best source book of history of Tamil Nadu during the Sangam age.

113.Ibid., 119 – 141
114.Ibid., 40 – 41
115. Ibid., 20
116. Ibid., 142 – 145
117. Ibid., 53
118. Ibid., 57
119. Ibid., 249
120. Ibid., 54
121. Ibid., 154 – 155
122. Ibid., 107
123.Ibid., 108

Chapter II

POLITICAL CONDITIONS OF THE TAMILS

The history of the Tamils may well be traced at least from the beginning of the Sangam era. The political history of the Sangam age also extends from the third century B.C. to third century A.D.

Perhaps the traditional order of saying Cera, Cola, Pandiya might have been arranged according to Tamil alphabetical order (சே. சோ. பா). The origin and development of these dynasties are yet to be discovered. Hence *Panniru Pattiyal* says that these Cera, Cola, Pandiya are the ancient dynasties.[124]

Ceras

The Cera country as it was situated on the western parts of South India, adjacent to Arabian Sea, was called 'Kutapulam' (Western place).[125] Vanci and Tonti were their interior and seashore capitals respectively, some scholars are of opinion that the cera dynasty may be the earliest of all the three dynasties for the following reason.

124. Panniru Pattiyal, 76
125. Cirupan. 1. 47.

According to the traditional order, Cera, Cola, Pandiya, Cera stands first; and *Tolkappiyam* as it speaks about the special garland or the floral of the trio, it mentions 'Pontai' (Palmyra) which belongs to Cera at first,[126] and hence the Cera dynasty may be the earliest but it seems rather tenuous.

We, with the help of *Patirruppattu* the poems of which speak exclusively of the Cera kings, can trace the Cera history of the Sangam age in order, at least for three generations. The order of the poems in *Patirruppattu* also is arranged in such a manner to give us a fairly connected account of the kings. The colophons at the end of each verse and the Vancikkantam of *Cilappatikaram* are very much useful for the formation of the chronological order of the Cera kings. The Cera kings in Sangam literature were called as Ceran, Ceralan, Atan, Kotai, kuttuvan, poraiyan and Irumporai. The Cera monarchs may be divided into two main groups namely the descendants of Utiyan Ceralatan and the descendants of Antuvan Ceral Irumporai.

There were marriage alliances between the Cera Kings and the Cola kings arid Velir families who were feudatories of Cola kings. For instance, Imayavarampan Netunceralatan married Narconai, the daughter of Cola king Manakkilli, and Utiyan Ceralatan married Nallini the daughter of Veliyan Venman, a Velir chieftain. However, hostility also prevailed among them. Imayavarampan Netuncerlatan and Verpakratakkai Peruvirarkilli, a Cola king, fought fiercely at Tirupporpuram, and both fell in the battlefield, leaving no one to claim victory. Some of the Cera kings were great poets also and Patal Patiya Perunkatunko and Marutam- patiya Ilankatunko are worth-mentioning.

126. Tol. Puram. 5.

PANDIYAS

Pandiyan dynasty is believed to be the oldest among the Tamil kings.

Mahavamsam states that Vijayan the first king of Ceylon married a Pandiya princess and be got Pantu vamca Teva.

Magasthenes and Kautilya mention the Pandiyan kingdom only.

Roman history assures about the Pandiyan envoy had been received in 20 B.C. by the great king Augustus Caeaar.

Roman copper coins are largely found aroung Madurai city. All these can support the antiquity of Pandiyan kingdom.

Pandiyan kingdom as it was situated on the southern parts of South India, or Tamilakam it was called as 'Tenpulam'[127] and the kings were called 'Tennavar'. Sangam literature mentions Madurai as Kutal. Madurai was the capital of Pandiyan kings and Korkai, which was famous for pearl fishery, was the sea-port, *Cilappatikaram* gives us a detailed account of the warfare machinaries fixed on the fortress of Madurai.[128]

Pandiya became most famous for the establishment of Tamil Sangam at Madurai and their patronage to poets; some kings themselves were renowned poets and their poems are included in the sangam literature.

Among the Pandiyas of the Sangam age, Palyakasalai Mutukutumi Peruvaluti seems to be the earliest. Purananuru calls

127. Cirupan. 63
128. Cilampu. 15/207-218

him as kutumi[129] and kutumi koman,[130] and hence it seems that his name might have been as kutumi. Purananuru describes him as a great hero, patron of poets, devotee of Siva and a performer of number of sacrifices. His grant of Velvikkuti a village to a Brahmin family was renewed by Pandiyan Netunoatalyan (675-690 A.D.) by his Velvikkuti Grant which gives an essential evidence about the Pandiyan King Mutukutumi of the Sangam age.

Ariyappatai Katanta Netunceliyan may be mentioned as the next important king. *Cilappatikaram* speaks about the victory over the Aryans,[131] but the details of the war are not known. He seems to be a poet too, and one of his poems about learning is included in the collection of *Purananuru.*[132] His name is connected with the story of Kovalan and Kanaki, and he died on the throne itself as soon as he learnt that Kovalan was innocent of the theft of the anklets of the Royal queen.

The most important Pandiyan ruler to be mentioned is Talaiyalankaattu Ceruvenra Pandiyan Netunceliyan. He assumed power as a ruler at his very early age. Hence the other two of the Trio, thought that the young Pandiyan king could be easily defeated and made alliance with Tirayan, Elini, Erumaiyuran and Porunan, and waged a war with Netunceliyan at Talaiyalankanam, in the north eastern part of his kingdom. But the young, energetic and valiant Netunceliyan fought fearlessly and took captive of the cera King Mantaran Ceral Irumporai and routed others completely. The great poet Mankuti Marutan who was patronized by Netunceliyan composed *Maturaikkanci*, the longest verse in *Pattuppattu*, with a view to weaning his ambitious and aggressive career

129. Puram. 6,9,12
130. Puram. 64
131. Cilampu. 23/14-18
132. Ibid. 23/183.

of conquest and to turn him into a peace-loving ruler, but it is ambiguous whether the king who -was also a poet, had followed the valuable advice.

COLAS

Cola kings ruled over the eastern part of Tamilakam and it was called 'Kunapulam.'[133] The Cola kings were called Cempiyan, Cenni, Valavan, etc. Asoka inscriptions speak about the Colas as the independent neighbours on the southern border of his empire. Anpil plates of Guntara Cola (956-976) and Kanniyakumari inscription of Vira Rajendra (1062 - 1069) and some other later inscriptions give creditable but scanty information about the early Colas. *Mahavamsam*, the history of Ceylon also often mentions the Cola kings as they had many political contacts since the time of Parantaka Cola I (907 - 955). The Colas claim that they belong to Solar origin as the Pandiyas are attributed to Lunar origin. The Cola kings Tunkeyil erinta Totittot Cempiyan, Cipi and Manu may be considered only as legendary kings. However, N. Subrahmanian contents that Elara of Mahavamsam may be identified with Manu who ruled from Tiruvarur because Elara was but a Ceylonese corruption of Alura Aruran), but it seems to be far-fetched.[134]

Uruvappakrer Ilancet Cenni, who ruled from Uraiyur, may be mentioned as the earliest Cola king of the Sangam age. Karikala the son of Ilancet Cenni, is the most distinguished and powerful among the Sangam Colas. The imperial Colas of Thanjavur and the Telugu Colas ruled from north of Tamilakam proudly claimed that they were the descendants of Karikalan and such was his power and greatness. Karika-

133. Cirupan. - 79
134. N. Subrahmanian, op.cit., pp. 73-74.

lan defeated the Cera monarch Perunceraldan, supported by a Pandiyan king and eleven velirs at the battle of Venni.[135] In another battle at the same Venni, he completely routed his enemies so as the whole of Tamilakam to accept his overlordship. Once he defeated nine minor princes at the battle of Vakaipparantalai. He had a powerful navy also, by which he conquered and established his rule in Ceylon.

Among the other Colas of the Sangam age, Kopperum Colan, whose friendship with the poet Picirantaiyar was given as an example for real friendship by commentators, was quite famous. Both of his sons rose against him, but on the intervening of the great poet Kovurkilar, he decided to end his life by fasting, which was called 'Vatakkiruttal'.

Pattinappalai introduces Tirumavalavan, the hero of the poem (Pattutait talaivan) as a young captive in the enemy's prison. As a tiger-cub with sharp claws had grown in a cage, he in the prison cell had grown in age as well as in strength and will-power, He, by calculated plan and with his unsheathed sword power, as a mighty tusker, trapped in a pit, broke the sides with its tusks and stepped on the piled earth, escaped and joined its mate, escaped and regained his crown.[136] From this, it is understandable that any one relative of the royal family with men-power, lost no opportunity to overthrow the ruling king and to seize the power and become the ruler, aid also it shows the unstable political condition of those days.

Pattinappalai gives us a fair list of conquests of Tirumavalavan but without any valuable information for the historical study. Not even the names of the enemy kings suffered defeat at the hands of Tirumavalavan are mentioned. Hence

135. Koyil Venni, 15 miles East of Thanjavur.
136. Pattina. 11. 210 - 217.

Pattinappalai is lack of evidence to show the kings and chieftains who were actually in the political arena and what were their real position but on the other spheres there is an enormous wealth of historical information.

Tirumavalavan subdued the Oliyar chiefs.[137] They were the chieftains of Olinatu which was one among the twelve neighbouring regions of Sentamilnatu. They were ponkarriatu, Olinatu, Tenpaivtinatu, Kuttanatu, Kutanatu, Karkanatu, Uitanatu, Pulinatu, Malainatu, Aruvanatu and Aruva Vatataiai natu.[138] These regions were situated from south-east to north-east of Sentamil natu. Hence this Olinatu might have been situated on the south of Colanatu.

Vidwan R. Raghava lyengar puts forth a more probable suggestion that according to Pudukkottai inscription No.145, this Olinatu may be identified with Olip parru, mentioned in the said inscription. This administrative division, Parru may be considered to be similar to the administrative division of Kottam or Kurram of the imperial Colas. The position of Olinatu also corroborates with the position of Olip Parru.[139]

The ancient Aruvalar of Aruvanatu, out of fear voluntarily offered their services to Tirumavalavan.[140] Aruva natu comprised the present southern part of Villupuram Taluk, Cuddalore, Chidambaram and Virutacalam Taluks. An inscription in the temple at Tiruvamattur reveals that Tiruvamattur was in the territory of Aruvanatu.[141]

(Olinatu) and northern (Aruvanatu) regions were mentioned so as to ensure that the other regions also were conquered by Tirumavalavan.

137. *Ibid.* 11.274
138. Tol. Col.400 Commentary
139. Critical Study of Pattinappalai, R. Raghava lyengar, p.94.
140. Pattina. 275.
141. M. Rajamaniokam, Op. cit, p.244.

The minor kings who ruled the territory to the north of Cola country were afraid of the invasion of Tirumavalavan.[142] Generally the term 'Vatavar' may mean the chieftains ruled the region north of Cola country. But, in this context scholars are of opinion that this term may mean the chieftains of Aruva Vatatalal Natu. According to the example verses given by Peraciriyar it may mean the Calukyas, whose emblem was pig.[143]

Kutavar that is the minor kings ruling over the regions west of Cola country also were subdued.[144] The term Kutavar may generally mean the cera, Kutaku (Coorg) and Konkar, and rather it is very vague. And even it may mean that the chieftains of Kutanatu, which is one among the twelve neighbouring regions and it is also on the west of Cola country.

Tirumavalavan subdued Tennavan also.[145] This term means beyond any doubt the Pandiyan king who was one of the three crown kings of Tamilakam. By these two expressions, we have to understand that both Cera and Pandiya kings were defeated by Tirumavalavan and were reduced to the status of feudatories.

Tirumavalavan completely destroyed the poduvar chiefs.[146] The term Potuvar generally means the shepherd but here it means the shepherd chiefs. It is clear that the shepherd tribe also was entitled to rule over some region or other. For instance Nandagopan the legendary king of shepherd community may be mentioned. But some scholars are of opinion that treacherous chiefs secretly engaged in conspiracy against the king were completely destroyed.

142. Pattina. 276.
143. Tol. Porul. Ceyyul. 146.
144. Pattina. 276.
145. *Ibid*, 277
146. *Ibid.*, 281

P.T.S. Iyengar says, "The word poduvar means herdsman chief and must refer to the rulers of the pastoral tribes that inhabited the Mullai region, north of Marutam lands, belonging to the Pallavas".[147]

Pattinappalai gives the conquest of Tirumavalavan over Irunkovel as the last one in the series.[148] Naccinarkkiniyar interprets the word 'Irunkovel' as 'Aimperu Velir' and they were Titiyan, Elini, Erumaiyuran, Irunkovenman and Porunan. But it seems according to Purananuru[149] that he was a king named Irunkovenman who ruled from Pidavur, which is identified with the present Pitavur in Ariyalur Taluk of Trichy District which was then within the cola territory.

Rajamanickam gives a version totally different. During the Sangam period, there was a town named Turavai, which he identifies with the Tvaracamutram in Mysore state (Karnataka), and it was ruled over by one Irunkovel. Kapilar, a great Sangam poet and a close friend of Pari, requested him to marry, both daughters of late pari, but it was not complied with.[150] Rajamanickam is under the impression that this Irunkovel is no other than the Irunkovel, who suffered a defeat at the hands of Tirumavalan. Hence Tirumavalavan annexed Mysore State also to the territory of his empire. This is also seems to be farfetched.

The elephants played an important and leading part in the battle on those days,[151] and the Royal elephant was given due respect by one and all, Cavalry and the infantry also did their part in the battle.[152]

147. P.T.Srinivasa Iyengar, Op.cit., p.346.
148. Pattina. 282.
149. Puram. 392
150. Puram. 201, 202
151. Pattina. 228 - 231.
152. *Ibid.*, 232

The soldiers attained martyrdom were honoured by erecting memorial stones over the graves of the fallen soldiers which were called 'natukal'.[153]

The pitiable condition of the enemy country after the defeat[154] was so horrible that no words could describe and was an exact evidence of the merciless acts of the kings of those days. Perhaps it might be due to the anger towards the enemy king, but it could not be fair, even it could be a cruel deed, to punish the subjects instead of the king.

However the captured Royal women folk, were given a fair and generous treatment which could be much appreciated They were engaged in the services of the temple, such as smearing the floor, decorating with flowers, and lighting the unquenched lamps there in the evening, etc.

Generally speaking there was no unity among the three crowned kings of Tamil Nadu, the tier a king at one time would join hands with Pandya king to defeat the Cola king.[155] At another time he could wage a war against the Pandiya king with the Cola monarch.[156] The feudatory chiefs like Malaiyamans who were actually the feudatories of Cola kings and expected to help them, also played the same game. Hence the political balance of Tamil Nadu was not stable during the Sangam age.

---

153. *Ibid.*, 79
154
155. Porunar. 142 - 148.
156. Akam. 116

Chapter III

SOCIAL CONDITIONS OF THE TAMILS

Literature is the most useful source of information for the social history of the Tamils of the Sangam age. The stray Tamil Brahmi inscriptions of the Pre-Sangam period give us very scanty information of the social life of the people of the Sangam period. We can gather valuable information from Pattinappalai about the social life, customs and habits of the ancient Tamils.

In spite of the five natural divisions of land or regions mentioned in Tamil literature, *Pattinappalai* confines only to Marutam and Neytal; because it speaks about Kavirippumpattinam, the then Cola capital city, and its surroundings. It is noticeable that the vast cola country was full of nearby hamlets.[157]

Social Order

The social order of the people was based either on the region in which they lived or on the occupation which they had adopted. The occupational or professional order in the long-run became birth-based. Among these, Vellala the agri-

157. Pattina. 28

culturist were highly respected by all other communities, as the daughters of Velir, the Vellala chiefs were given in marriage to the Tamil kings; and the merchant community which was the backbone of national economy also emerged from this social order.

The Vellalas are introduced as Ulavar (Cultivator) who own the curved plough and led a virtuous life with gracious love. They condemn killing and abhor stealing; perform their duties to the heavenly gods and offer oblations; rear cow and bull with much care exalt the priests who learned the four vedas and distributed food cooked and uncooked.[158] In the above passage incidentally the Brahmin community is mentioned.[159]

We next see the prosperous merchant community, which is believed to be an offshoot of the Vellalas. As the long yoke of a plough is balanced by a central pin, their heart is poised and just. They won't take anything more than what should they get, and won't give anything less than what they should give and thus they regard the goods of others equal to that of their own. They announce the profit openly and sell goods. The wealth they possess now was acquired by such a just and proper way.[160] There was no dispute in the trade, and their commercial morality seems to have been based on a higher principle than 'business is business'.

In Tami Nadu the Kshatriya community was nowhere in the picture in those days. The kings and the merchants were not different from the agriculturists, but the traditional occupation alone had distinguished them.

158. *Ibid.* 199-205
159. *Ibid.* 202
160. *Ibid.* 206-212

Jains and Buddhists

By mentioning the hermitages[161] the author indicates that there were Jains and Buddhists in Tamil Nadu then. It may be mentioned here that Asoka sent a mission of *Dharmamahamatras* to Ceylon via South India, which had its impact on the Tamils also. But even earlier Badrabahu and his ascetic followers came and settled at Mysore. Hence it will be probable to say that a fair number of Jains and Buddhists were in Tamil Nadu during the Sangam age. Scholars are of opinion that due to the impact of Jainism and Buddhism on the people of North India the Brahmins had no other alternative but to migrate to South India. However the reference in Pattinappalai about the Brahmin ascetics or sages with bright matted locks and their sacrifices ensure that the Brahmins in Tamil Nadu then led a peaceful life and performed their religious duties without any obstruction. The kings also openly favoured their sacrifices.

Foreign Merchants

Foreign merchants from Rome, Greece, Sri Lanka, Burma and China were carrying on an extensive trade with Tamilakam during the Sangam age. Muciri, Korkai and pukar were the main seaports of the Cera, Pandiya and Cola kings respectively; among which Pukar was the foremost during the reign of Tirumavalavan. The foreign traders came to Pukar very often and even had their own settlement there. Arikkametu one such settlement near Pondicherry may well prove this. In spite of their different languages they led a happy and peaceful life in Pukar.[162]

161. *Ibid.* 53m tavappalli
162. Pattina. 216-217; Cilampu. 5/10-12

Foreign merchants of the west is mentioned in Sangam literature as Yavanas.[163] This term yavanas were applied first to Greeks, then to the Romans and later to all foreigners. The South Indian merchants and other employed yavanas on some special jobs in which they were well trained. The Roman soldiers were enlisted in the army of certain Pandiyan kings. Ariyappatai katanta Netunceliyan had employed Yavanas to be the guards of his palace.[164] *Mullaippattu* reveals that the language of the Yavanas was unintelligible to the Tamils and hence they were obliged to us gestures.[165] Perumpanarrup-patai speaks about the remarkable skills of the yavanas in making the artistic and ornamental brass lamps.[166]

All these people mentioned here belong to Pattinappa-kkam or the capital city of Kavirippumpattinam.

Paratavar

Kavirippumpattinam was the coastal city and hence the suburban area of the city also was in the coastal region. In those days the coastal region was called 'neytal' and Varunan the sea-God was prescribed to that region.[167] It was so called after the Neytal flower which grewabundantly in the back-waters of that region. The natural occupation of the coastal region was fishing and the people who had adopted fishing as their occupation was called 'minavar' after the Tamil word 'min' that is the people who lived on fishing. They were also called as 'Paradavar'.[168] They were mentioned in the Sangam literature as 'Valainar'[169] and 'nulaiyar'.[170]

163. Akam. 149, Puram 56
164. Cilambu. 14/66-67
165. Mullaippattu 65-66
166. Perumpan. 316-317
167. Tol. Akattinai lyal 5.
168. Pattina. 90 and 112.
169. *Ibid*. 197; Puram249/3; Maturaikkanci 256;
170. Akam 363/11

In the early days they earned their livelihood by fishing near the sea-coast and selling them on the spot itself. In due course they used to go far into the sea for fishing and took their commodity to the interior parts of the country and bartered them for other kinds of foodstuffs. In the beginning they went into the sea by using the primitive kind of canoe that is binding the logs together to form a float namely a 'kattumaram' which is in use even at present. Later they built boats small and big and carried on their trade along the sea-coasts. Gradually they became sailors, who took their trade to Arabia and Africa in the West, and Burma and China in the East. *Perumpanarruppatai* speaks about their large houses in the broad streets approaching the seashore.[171] *Pattinappalai* indicates that those paratavar who went into the far sea for fishing, used to find their ways by counting the bright lamps burning throughout night on the terraces of the large houses on the seashore.[172]

Status of Women

The treatment of women in *Pattinappalai* is highly commendable. In the text we find references to the young maids with shining forehead and guiltless look are entrusted to watch the drying grains in front of the spacious houses. They unmindingly scare away the guilt fowls by throwing away their golden ear-ring[173]. This shows clearly the gold ornaments were in much use among the Tamils during the Sangam age and also they were very rich.

On the full moon day, which is specially intended for Varunan the sea-God, the dark skinned paratavar folk, neglected their usual work of fishing in the wide cold sea, ate

171. Perupan. 322-324
172. Pattina 112.
173. Ibid 20 – 23.

and drank, and enjoyed playing with their black mates, who wore garments of green leaves[174].

This reminds us in the ancient days, women used to wear around their waist green leaves plaited with colourful flowers. This kind of fanciful attire was considered a decorative garment,[175] and was used by maids, on extraordinary occasions such as festivals. And it is evident that the full moon day was set apart for offering prayers to Varunan the sea-God by the Paradavar folk; hence their womenfolk presented with garment of foliage. This kind of scanty clothing was sometimes mistaken to be complete nudity by the foreigners like Strabo[176].

Late at night due to excess of joy and drowsiness, both husband and his consort were not in their usual senses and habits. She instead of wearing her silk saree wore the white cloth of her husband; instead of taking her usual soft drink drank the sweet alcoholic drink intended for her husband; and adorned herself with kanni the garland prepared for her husband, and in the same way her husband wore kotai the garland intended for his consort[177].

It is evident, in those days both men and women used to drink but the drinks were quite different from each other; the women used to wear silk, but the men were contended with cotton. It is noteworthy that the garland of men was much different from that of women, with different names kanni and kotai.

In connection with the festival of 'Gev vel', the maid possessed with Murukan dances in the broad street, of Pukar,

174. Ibid 90 – 93.
175. Narrinai 123/7; Akam 70/12, Ainkurunuru 22/1-2.
176. K. K. Pillay, "*Social History of Tamils*", Univ. of Madras, 1975, p. 300.
177. Pattina. 106 - 110.

amidst the thickly crowded people of Pukar and its neighbourhood, and she is dancing to the tune of flute and lute and the timing sounds of drums and tabors. In order to witness the dance and worship Lord Murukan the fair coral like complexioned ladies gather on the upstairs and peep through the windows. Their feet are pink and their attractive waists are adorned with guads of gold; they are arrayed like peacock's gay with their deer like eyes, their speech is sweeter than the parrot's prattling; they worship Lord Murukan with folded hands full of bangles. Which look like the sprouted cluster of kantal flowers.[178]

The beautiful ladies are portrayed with coral like fair complexion; hence the view of a few historians that the ancient Tamils were black holds no good. If the fishermenfolk is presented with dark skin, it is due to their exposure to the hot sun all day long. The ladies gather on the upstairs and worship Murukan with their folded hands. This establishment that the Murukan worship was prevalent during the Sangam age.

Murukan Worship

The Murukan festival reminds us that Lord Murukan was doubtless the pre-eminent God of Tamils through the ages. The word 'murukul, the root of Murugan, denotes beauty, youth, God, etc. besides Murukan himself,[179] and this suggests that the ancient Tamils had associated their God with the permanent youth and beauty reflected in Nature. Nallantuvanar, a Sangam poet, says that Murukan is the lord of the seven worlds.[180] The 'vel' (spear) is his favourite weapon, and from its name he is called 'Velan' even his priest is called 'Velan' and

178. Ibid 146 – 155.
179. Kuru. 362/1
180. Paripatal 8/64

the dance performed by him (the priest) in connection with the worship of Murukan also was known as 'Velan Teriyatal'.[181] It is evident from our text, that there were women priests also and they too performed the veriyatal by which they were called 'veriyatu makalir'.

Konti Makalir

The women prisoners of wars, especially members of the royal family were given a fair and courteous treatment, and this can be said to be the most appreciable act of Tirumavalavan. They were called 'Konti Makalir' that is taken as was prisoners. These konti makalir were entrusted to light the unquenched lamps at the temples in the evening, after taking their bath in the tank used for drinking.[182] It is evident that the women captives in those days were given fair treatment and due respect.And it is also understandable that no one should take bath in a tank set apart for drinking but these konti makalir were allowed to do so, as they were engaged in the services of the holy temples.

Vidvan Raghava lyengar confuses this konti makalir of Pattinappalai with the konti makalir of *Manimekalai*[183] and concludes that this konti makalir is no other than those of pathiyilar who are put in the services of the temples; and in support of his interpretation, he shows a line of *Tevaram*[184] also. The konti makalir of *Pattinappalai* clearly denotes the women of the Royal family taken as prisoners of war, but the konti makalir of *Manimekalai,* beyond any doubt, denotes the parattaiyar (harlots) who takes money from persons who are in need of pleasure. It is ununderstandable whether Ra-

181. Kuru. 360/1
182. Pattina. 246-247
183. Manimekalai 18/109
184. Tevaram 710/7

ghava Iyengar had noticed the wide difference between the parattaiyar and Patiyilar (devadasis). Parattaiyar who were considered as outcaste 'kotai kali makalir'[185] by Ilanko Atikal, were not entitled to undertake the services of temples, and in the same way patiyilar are not intended to practice prostitution but to render temple services. Further the system of devadasis was not prevalent in Tamil Nadu earlier that, the seventh century A.D, and there is no evidence to show that the devadasis had adopted prostitution in the early period. In view of the above facts the interpretation of Raghava Iyengar for konti makalir stands invalid.

Slavery

There is neither directly nor indirectly any trace of slavery in *Pattinappalai*; but it is traceable in some other classics. *Kalittokai* reveals that there was a peculiar practice by which the slaves were branded on the chest.[186]

Megasthenes said that slavery as an institution was never known to India; as he had never seen an open market for the sale of slaves.

V. Kanakasabai says, "Slavery was ever unknown amongst the Tamils and this is strong evidence of their superior civilization in the early period."[187] V.A. Smith also remarks "slavery is said to have been unknown amongst the Tamils."[188]

But N. Subramaniyam concludes in a reasonable way that there might have been slavery in Tamilakam but in disguise. He puts forth the following in support of his view: *Purana-*

185. Cilappatikaram 14/71
186. Kalittokai 84/26-27
187. V. Kanakasabai, Op. cit., p.114.
188. V.A. Smith, op.cit., p.411

nuru merit ions the term 'atiyurai' which means 'atmai'.[189] *Cilappatikaram* mentions the term 'Urimaci Curram' which means 'atimai' since the footnote says 'atimaittiral'. Tirutton-tar Puranam mentions directly the word 'atimai'.[190]

These evidences seem to be proper and appropriate. He also says that unconditional submission of a subject to the king, of a disciple to his guru and of the wife to her husband also indicate the slavery in a philosophical way.[191]

In addition to these things the system of bonded labour that is 'pannaiyal' system which existed till recently may be considered as an evidence.

However we have to give margin that there is no direct evidence in the Sangam classics to show that there existed the institution of slavery.

Food

Rice and Millet The diet system of the ancient Tamils was not much different from that of the present days.

Primarily it may depend upon the flora and fauna of the land. The diet of the Tamils was simple but a great importance was attached to it, as it is the life sustainer. They thought that hunger is the worst enemy of mankind[192]. Hence it was said that he who provided food was he who gave the life.[193] Cooked rice was the staple food of the ancient Tamils and it continued through the ages without much change. Hence *Pattinappalai* begins with the fertile paddy fields and the river Kaviri which makes the Cola country prosperous.

189. Puram 67/12
190. Tatuttatkonta Puranam, stanza 37 & 40
191. N. Subramanian, op.cit., pp.296-297, 345-346
192. Puram 136-140
193. Manimekalai 11/96

The river Kaviri which will never cease to flow, even though the rain fails, starts from the mountain top and flows into the sea and makes the country rich by its mineral mingled water.[194] Unlike some prominent rivers in India, such as the Tungabhadra in the south and Jamuna in the north, Kaviri flows directly into the sea. Further it is noteworthy that Kaviri has not changed its course, anyway for the past two thousand years and more and continued to contribute to the prosperity of the Cola country through the ages.

There are vast paddy fields with one crop or the other always.[195] The land is cultivated throughout the year with alternative crop plants. Paddy is mentioned twice in the poem,[196] but no other grain has found a place anywhere in the poem. This clearly shows that the rice was the main foodstuff of the ancient Tamils. Perhaps, the marutam region in which Pukar and the interior surroundings were situated, may be another reason for the omission, as paddy was the chief crop of marutam.

In those days rice, whether raw or boiled, was prepared by pounding in a mortar with a pestle.[197] No reliable evidence is available to show that the ancient Tamils used metallic vessels for cooking. Prior to cooking generally the rice was cleansed and the pebbles and such other things were removed. It also seems that rice was cooked even without cleansing.[198] The rich people used to take cooked rice with sumptuous accessories.

There is ample evidence from Sangam classics to show that milk was in use, and sometimes the rice was cooked with

194. Pattina. 11. 5.7.
195. *Ibid.* 8
196. *Ibid.* 13; 'kaicennel' 240, 'ceonel'
197. Cirupan. 193-194
198. *Ibid.* 98-100

milk.[199] Curd and buttermilk also had their due places in the meals and they were very popular in those days too. Ghee was used invariably by the middle and high class people. It is needless to say that plenty of Ghee was used in the performance of sacrifices. As an evidence to these things, *Pattinappalai* mentions cattle rearing[200] (cow and bull). Goats milk and curd prepared out of it also were used by some people.[201]

Sugarcane

Sugarcane had played a prominent part in the life of ancient Tamils. It is considered as a twin agricultural product with paddy as both of these only are cultivated in the wetland. Hence the author puts them together in the poem twice.[202] There are numerous references in the sangam classics about the sugarcane and its various uses. *Pattinappalai* speaks that there were sugarcane presses and jaggery was prepared out of the boiled sugarcane juice. Sugarcane juice was also taken as a soft drink. *Kuruntokai* reveals that there was a custom of drawing the figure of sugarcane on the broad shoulder of women.[203] Sugarcane flower has been used as a smile in many places on various aspects in Sangam classics.

Uruttirankannanar compared the white flags waving on the pole attached to the curved bar on the locked baskets of tasty victuals kept for sale, to the waving white flowers of the sugarcane grown alnong the wild river.[204]

---

199. Malai. 417
200. Pattina. 201
201. Pattina 8-9, 240
202. Kuru. 221
203. Kuru. 384.
204. Pattina 111 - 118

Akananuru speaks about a feast provided to panar; in that feast mutton roasted in the fire and cooked tinai rice (millet) were served. Aval (beaten rice or rice flakes) cooked in the sugarcane juice and milk was also served.[205]

Vellaikkuti Nakanar compares the white waving flowers of sugarcane to the appearance of a group of spears.[206]

Sumptuous and tasty food was consumed by rich people in cities. *Pattinappalai* reveals that various kinds of sweet meats and tasty victuals were prepared and consumed by ancient Tamils.[207]

Besides rice, other grains such as maize and other millets also were used. The maize and millets were prominent in the hilly and forest regions that is kurinci and mullai, while the rice dominated marutam, the agricultural region. Kollu (horse gram)[208] and katalai (Bengal gram)[209] also are mentioned in Sangam classics. The poor people had to take greens such as vallai,[210] velai,[211] kuppaikkirai[212] etc.

Fruits and Vegetables

Pattinappalai gives a foremost place to paddy as the rice is the main item of the daily food of the Tamils. However the fruits and vegetables also had their due status in the dietary of the Tamils. *Pattinappalai* mentions the following trees and plants which were popular and available in abundance;

205. Akam 237
206. Puram 35/9-10
207. Pattina. 163-164
208. Puram 105
209. *Ibid.* 120
210. Ibid. 16
211. Ibid. 246
212. Ibid. 159

and they are also found mention in other Sangam classics as well. Plantain,[213] mango,[214] kamuku,[215] (arecanut) coconut,[216] palmyrah,[217] cempu,[218] (Indian kales plant), turmeric[219] and inci (medicinal ginger plant).[220]

Jack fruit, the most important and one of the fruits trio, that is mukkani, has not a place in *Pattinappalai* but it is mentioned in the other Sangam works.[221]

Different kinds of fruits such as plantain, mango, jack-fruit and other delicious fruits were consumed as such or mixed with sugar, honey or milk. Tender coconut juice was a much desired drink and it too was mixed with other sweet substances and consumed.

Among the wide variety of fruits the plantain, jack fruit and mango were highly esteemed. Ilantai (gooseberry), naval (Eugenia jambolana), sweet tamarind and palmyrah fruits were popular among the poor. The tamarind tree is mentioned in *Narrinai.*[222]

Vegetables were used to prepare sauces and consumed with cooked rice or any other grain cooked. In those days also a fair number of vegetables might have been used but no details are available. *Patirruppattu* mentions beans among the accessories. It is also notable that beans was used independently as food or accessories.[223] Sometimes vegetables were

213. Pattina. 16; Kuru. 308/1
214. Ibid 17; Kuru 331/6
215. Ibid 17; Netunal 237; Patirru. 7
216. Ibid 16; Puram 61/9; Patirru. 13/7
217. Ibid 18, 74, 89; kuru 177/3
218. Ibid. 19; perumpan. 361; Malai. 343
219. Ibid 19; Maturai. 289
220. Ibid 17; Sirupan. 44; Malai. 343
221. Kurun. 376/6 patirru. 61/1; puram 200/1-2
222. Narrinai 314/3
223. Puram 335/5-6; Perumpan. 95-96

fried in oil.[224] Pickles prepared out of tender mangoes also was in use.[225]

It is clear from Sangam classics that fish and meat had a prominent part in the diet of the ancient Tamils.[226] The Sangam poets enthusiastically praised the meat dishes and the relish derived from them. We learn from *Purananuru* that hare and other tender animals were roasted and eaten.[227] *Malaipatukatam* reveals that the flesh of ram, deer,[228] hare, fowl, porcupine, pig and boar was used as food. The meat and fish were sometimes either dried or roasted or fried and used. Fish was used abundantly by the people of coastal region as well as the people of interior parts of the country. Generally the dried and preserved fish was used by the people who lived away from the coastal region.

Pattinappalai reveals that paratavar ate the roasted fish (iral caught from the sea) and the others ate the fried flesh of field tortoise.[229] We learn from the same poem that the fish was cut into pieces and fried and used.[230]

Before concluding this, we have to consider one more relevant and important point regarding the food habits of the ancient Tamils. It is certain that all the Tamils of the Sangam age might have been non-vegetarians as almost all the Sangam poets speak about the various preparations of the meat and fish consumed by the people. However we have to infer that there might have been a fair number of vegetarians also.

224. Ibid. 127
225. Perumpan. 355
226. Patirru. 29/4-5; puram 342/10; 14/12; perumpan.282; Porunar. 105
227. Puram 319/8
228. Malai. 175
229. Pattina. 63-64
230. *Ibid.* 176-177

Pattinappalai ascertains this by presenting the temples or hermitages of Jains and Buddhists.[231] Both of them, especially Jains taught strict vegetarianism by prohibiting the killing of any one, either human of animal or bird or even the small insects. *Tirukkural* and otheir didactic - works such as Nalatiyar also might have influenced the people to adopt vegetarianism. Hence it can be well determined that vegetarianism had its offshoot in Tamil Nadu even during the Sangam period.

Drink

There is no doubt that toddy of various kinds was very popular during the Sangam age and they figured prominently, especially on festive occasions.[232] It is needless to say that the kings and chieftains of Tamil Nadu had a great pleasure in. providing the poets, bards and other dignitaries who attended to his court, with roasted meat and delicious drink. There is a large number of references, in the Sangam classics to the common use of toddy and different varieties of toddy. They are mentioned in different names. Patinappalai mentions four different kinds of toddy with different names such as pili,[233] mattu,[234] matu[235] and naravu.[236] Toddy is referred in other Sangam classics as kal,[237] teral,[238] pili,[239] naravu,[240] mattu[241]and matu[242] and these references may well prove the ex-

231. *Ibid.* 53
232. puram 129/1-3
233. attina, 89
234. *Ibid.* 108
235. Ibid. 180
236. Ibid 180
237. Puram 68/15;
238. Ibid. 97/14, Porunar. 157, kuru. 330/5
239. perumpan. 281
240. Puram 297/6, Kuru. 394/2
241. Ibid. 396/16
242. Porunar. 217

tensive use of the various kinds of toddy by people. Generally toddy was prepared from the juice' drained from the spathe of either coconut or palmyra. Toddy was distilled from millets also. A more popular intoxicating kind of drink was the fermented juice of palmyra. Teral was the distilled and concentrated kind of toddy.[243] Juice extracted from sugarcane and certain flowers was used as a mild drink.[244] Tender coconut juice was an enjoyable drink, free from any kind of intoxicating effects.

It is notable that women too were indulged in drinking but of a mild variety.[245] *Patinappalai* reveals the women who were with their mates, at the last quarter of the night, instead of taking mattu which was intended for them, drank matu kept for their husbands. Hence it is clear that the women used to take a sweet kind of drink free from any kind of intoxicating effect, but the men used to drink a variety of more intoxicating drink.

Dress

Sangam classics refer to various kinds of dress of those days. The dress should be suitable to the region and climate and also the economical condition of the individual concerned. As Tamil Nadu is in the tropical region there is no need either for too much of cotton dress or of woollen. Hence the cotton dress was more popular among all Tamils and the silk also was in use, perhaps by the rich, *Pattinappalai* contains very scanty reference about the dress of those days. It speaks about the cotton, silk and foliage dresses. It says that the ladies by mistake were the cottono, cloth of their husbands in-

243. Akam. 2/4
244. *Ibid.* 160/11
245. Perumpan. 386-387

stead of their own silk sarees.[246] It shows that the silk was used invariably by ladies and the ancient Tamils were well trained in fine cotton weaving and in silk too. *Pattinappalai* mentions also about the use of foliage dress by the paratavar women.[247] This is clear evidence to show that in ancient times the foliage dress was in use among the maids and ladies on festive and ceremonial occasions.

Ornaments

Ornaments were very popular among the ancient Tamils and there were numerous varieties of them and especially the married women were crazy for such ornaments. But one should not think that all the maids and ladies were all kinds of ornaments mentioned in Sangam classics. Particular ornament worn by particular individual depended on the social and economical conditions of the person concerned. *Pattinappalai* provides no details of ornaments worn by ancient Tamils, and it refers wherever necessary by the common term ilai (ornament), such as nerilai[248] (proper ornament), pasilai[249] (special or gold ornament) and murrilai[250] (complete set of ornaments). Ilai is a common name for the ornaments as they are made of gold and studded with diamonds. However mention is made about two particular ornaments namely kulai[251] and toti.[252] Kulai means an ear ring but here the 'kotunkulai' may be said as an ear ornament such as modern 'jimikki' and 'pon toti' means in this context may mean the golden bracelet as it is worn by putalvar (sons).

246. Pattina. 107
247. *Ibid.* 96
248. *Ibid* 22
249.*Ibid* 147
250. *Ibid* 296
251. *Ibid* 23
252. *Ibid* 295

House

Primitive men lived in the natural caves, and worshipped Nature via. Sun, Moon, Cloud and even Lightning. But in course of time he felt the need of a dwelling place as much as that of food drink and clothing, arid gradually he began to build houses so as to protect himself from the horrors of the sun, Rain and even cruel animals etc.

No doubt the Sangam classics reveal that the ancient Tamils were far advanced in thief aspect too. They were well trained in the art of brick and mortar. We hear about the cloud capped storeyed buildings of pukar from Pattinappalal.[253]

Pattinappalai speaks of the large houses with spacious front-yards.[254] They used to have double doors.[255] Invariably, the royal buildings had the tiger mark, the royal emblem of the Cola kings.[256] There were small tanks and cattle sheds in the spacious frontyard of the large houses.[257]

There were huge and lofty steyed buildings with many halls big and small with a narrow passage between the main entrance and the next inside door; and there were much elevated pials around the buildings which were provided with long ladders with close set rungs.[258] There were windows to allow the breeze in.[259] Pattinappalai speaks about the storeyed buildings with huge circular pillars, where numerous guests were fed in the spacious kitchen halls and the surplus

253. Pattina. 145
254. *Ibid.* 20
255. *Ibid.* 40
256. *Ibid.* 40
257. *Ibid.* 51-52
258. *Ibid.* 142-145
259. *Ibid.* 151

was kept ready for the newcomers.[260] It is also said that there were grain stores in the interior parts of houses.[261]

Customs and Habits

The young girls were entrusted with watching the drying grains in front of their houses as they were not engaged otherwise.[262] Perhaps this may remind us that the young maids were sent to the tinai (millet) field for watching the ear of corn (katir) which naturally led them to the pre-marital love (kalavu).

The three-wheeled tiny cars pushed by young boys would be barredby the 'kulai'(ear ornament) thrown at the fowls.[263] This may reveal that the use of inatai vanti' three-wheeled cart, of these days which enables the children to walk werein use in those days.

Paddy was received in exchange of salt.[264] This shows the existence of barter system in those days, and the paddy was used as a measure of value. Even in the early part of this century the hawkers used to sell vegetables etc. in exchange of paddy in the villages of Thanjavur district.

The thick dust raised by the running chariots stained the beautiful pictures painted on the white walls of the palace.[265] This shows clearly that in those days the palace vails were white and painted with various kinds of beautiful pictures.

The people from the coastal region wore the flowers of atampu - a creeper on the sandy land and the people from

260. *Ibid.* 261-262.
261. *Ibid.* 267.
262.*Ibid.* 20-24.
263. *Ibid.* 24-25.
264. *Ibid.* 29-30.
265. *Ibid.* 47-50.

other (marutam) region wore the flowers of water-lily.[266] This reveals that in those days flowers of various kinds adorned the heads of men and women alike. It is also learnt from Pattinappalai that the bloom of sheathed-pine was worn[267] as well as the garland of venkutalam (ventali).[268]

Incidentally, 'natukal' is mentioned in a context of a simile.[269] This reveals that in those days a tomb stone or memorial stone called 'natukal' was erected in honour of a warrior who fell in the battle field.[270]

In those days flags were used for various purposes. The sacred flag at the temple's gate was adorned by all;[271] the white banner at the pole top on the basket of tasty victuals served as a sign of sale;[272] another imposing flag called upon the learned for discussion on various lores;[273] the flags on the masts of the ships anchored in the port at Pukar, announced to which nation they belongs[274] and the flag at the entrance of toddy shops told the people about the sale and pice of toddy.[275]

It is also notable that white rice was strewn on the baskets of sweetmeats as an oblation[276] fried fish and meat were sold at the noisy entrance of the toddy shops and flowers were strewn on the heaped sands in front of them.[277]

---

266. *Ibid.* 65-66.
267. *Ibid.* 88.
268. *Ibid.* 85.
269. *Ibid.* 79.
270. puram 221/13
271 Pattina
272.
273.
274. *Ibid.* 79.
275. *Ibid.* 180.
276. *Ibid.* 165.
277. *Ibid.* 176-178.

Soldiers of Tirumavalavan who rose against the enemy king wore the flowers of pulai and ulinai.[278] Wearing the particular flower by the army in action was a traditional and meaningful custom of war adopted by the ancient Tamils; and the particular flower they wore itself would reveal the particular action of war they had taken. The pulai flower was generally worn as a mark of heroism, and hence it adorns the war drum, ulinai is the name of the particular flower as well as the name of a particular main division of Purattinai which is chiefly related to war and its activities. The term ulinai is meant for besieging and capturing the enemy's fort,[279] and the army involved in this action would wear the ulinai flower. Hence it is meant, in this context that the army of Tirumavalavan rose to besiege and

Capture the fort of enemy king

Once the parrots were prattling sweetly from the elevated pials of the white walled houses; but now the bent-billed owls, even in the daylight are hooting from the empty grain stores, as the hunters wearing chappals came with their small drums and bows, and plundered the stock.[280] This reveals that in ancient times, the high class ladies used to tend beautiful parrots as a hobby fed them with milk and fruits and enjoyed their pleasant prattling and also we have to infer that the chappal was in use among the ancient Tamils.

The fishermen in the sea, late at night used to count the bright lamps on the storeys of the lofty houses in Pukar and located their alighting places.[281] Hence the houses in Pukar were so lofty as to be used as light houses.

278. *Ibid.* 235.
279. Tol. Purattinai 10
280. Pattina. 263-268
281. *Ibid.* 111-112.

In those days tiger mark, the royal emblem of the Cola king was stamped on the tax paid goods-bags. This shows the regular working of the custom houses which formed part of the well established cola administration.

Sports and Pastimes

The ancient Tamils had their own sports and pastimes which revealed their rustic simplicity and refinement. Generally the kings and chieftains enjoyed their leisure time by listening to the poems and songs of the poets and the bards respectively. They provided the poets and the ministrels with rich feast and costly dress and even with valuable gifts. The rich ladies in Pukar, enjoyed their leisure time by bringing up parrots and hearing their prattling.[282] The elites of the capital city enjoyed music and witnessed plays during their leisure times,[283] and some others enjoyed the pleasures of the pleasant moonlight night.[284] Some of the fishermen, at their leisure time caught the crabs and caused them to dance, and some others plunged into the rolling waves of the might sea and dabbled; and some more other took pleasure in puppet fashioning.[285]

Pattinappalai presents a vivid description of a contest held at Pukar in a spacious and raised ground provided for the purpose. The people from the neytal region and marutam region gathered there and contesting men too arrived in the scene and mingled with the commons, as the ever bright planets in the blue sky are mixed with the shining stars. The wrestling contest began first and wielding contest using quarter staff as well as sword followed next. But no one

282. *Ibid.* 294.
283. *Ibid.* 113.
284. *Ibid.* 114.
285. *Ibid.* 101-102.

in any of these contests became victorious. Hence they began to try their strength by throwing stones from the slings which scared the birds staying on the age long and tall palmyra trees.[286]

This clearly shows that the sports of the ancient Tamils were simple but at the same time meant to improve their strength so as to enable them to serve the Royal force.

286. *Ibid* 67-74

Chapter IV

ECONOMIC CONDITIONS OF THE TAMILS

Occupation

Agriculture

During the Sangam age and even afterwards agriculture was the main occupation of the Tamils. In the beginning the people cultivated some coarse varieties of paddy and other grains such as millets. Gradually the methods of cultivation had improved and during the sangam age, it had become well developed. The agriculturists in Tamil Nadu had maintained a respectable status among the people. *Tirukkural*, the scripture of the Tamils, praises the nature and importance of agriculture in an entire chapter.

Agriculture alone can save the mankind from the pangs of hunger and hence almost all the people have to depend either directly or indirectly on agriculturists. Generally the agriculturists alone can be generous as they have a good stock of grains always with them and the word 'velanmai' which denoted agriculture first, later denoted the hospitality. Hence *Pattinappalai* speaks in detail about the public feeding twice.[287] Ilanko Atikal says that the appeasement of the man's appetite and the sustenance of the king's prowess depend on the agriculture.[288]

Major part of the Cola country was wet land as it was watered by the overflowing Kaviri. Pattinappalai says that cultivation was going on throughout the year without any interval, and hence the fields were always with one crop or the other.[289] However the first preference was given to paddy cultivation which yielded an enormous and surplus return. *Pattinappalai* reveals this fact by mentioning the paddy thrice,[290] the rice once,[291] cooked rice in large measure twice,[292] the spacious kitchen halls as well as the feeding of numerous persons twice[293] and the grain stores twice.[294]

This enormous yield of paddy helped the people to be self-sufficient in food, their vital need; and the surplus grains helped them to get sufficient money for their other necessary expenses and also improved their economic condition to some extent, besides improving the economic condition of the country also.

Sugarcane

Being the twin agricultural product of wet land *pattinappalai* presents the sugarcane next.[295] It mentions both paddy and

287. Pattina. 43-45; 261-262
288. Cilampu 10/148-150
289. Pattina. 8
290. *Ibid.* 13, 130,240.
291. *Ibid.* 165
292.*Ibid.* 43,262
293. *Ibid.* 15, 26.
294. *Ibid.* 43, 262
295. *Ibid.* 9

sugarcane together twice.[296] The sugarcane is also mentioned in the same text as a simile.[297] Both paddy and sugarcane are the best examples to show the fertility of the land as well as they are the best sources of income. There are numerous references in the Sangam classics about the sugarcane and its various uses.[298]

Pattinappalai reveals that there were sugarcane presses, where the juice was boiled and jaggery and sugar were prepared. The fragrant smoke coming out of the boiling juice, made the lily flowers grown in the nearby fields, to grow pale and fade.[299] This shows that the ancient Tamils were carrying on this industry as one of the main cottage industries which yielded them much profit.[300] *Patirruppattu* says that the sugarcane harvest was going on throughout the year.[301] The same literature reveals a peculiar use of sugarcane. That is the bulk of sugarcane was used as a float.[302] Purananuru and *Ainkurunuru* reveal that there were sugarcane presses.[303] Hence the cultivation of sugarcane also was certainly a means to improve the economic condition of the agriculturists.

Cattle Rearing

Cattle is closely connected with agriculture. Bulls and Buffaloes are much needed for agriculture. Besides this the milk and the milk-products are used as food. So the cattle rearing is very essential to any country. In those days their were a

296. *Ibid.* 8-9
297. *Ibid.* 162
298. Akam 6/8; Puram 322/7; Kuru.85/4; Patirru. 30/14; Ainkuru 55/1; Pari 7/55,
299. Pattina. 9-12
300. Patirru. 75/6
301. *Ibid.* 30/14
302. *Ibid.* 87/4
303. Puram 322/7; Ainkuru. 55/1

separate class of people set apart for the purpose. They were called antar,[304] ayar,[305] itaiyar,[306] kovals[307] and potuvar.[308] Their main occupation was dairy farming and other allied works which provided their livelihood. This shows that cattle-rearing also was one of the important occupations of the ancient Tamils. In these days the term cowherd means the person who looks after cows and bulls and term shepherd means a person one who tend the sheeps and goats; but in those days the terms mentioned above were used only as common terms. It seems however that the term kovalar denoted only cowherds. Perhaps this might have been derived from the word 'gopalar' (the protector of cows) and it is noteworthy that Lord Krishna is mentioned as Kovalan.[309] We see in Pattinappalai, buffalo,[310] bull,[311] bullocks,[312] cows[313] and male-sheep (takar)[314].

From this we have to infer that the cattle-rearing was considered as an essential occupation. The sale of milk and milk-products helped the people improve their economic condition.

Weaving

Weaving was the next important occupation of the people. There is no doubt that a remarkable measure of skill in weaving had been achieved by the Tamils of the Sangam age. They were able to produce fine and super-fine varieties of cotton

304. Kuru. 117/3 21
305. Puram 300/17
306. Perumpan 175
307. Akam 14/7
308. Pattina 281
309. Pari 3/83
310. Pattina 14
311. *Ibid* 201
312. *Ibid 52,* 201
313. *Ibid* 201
314. *Ibid 77, 141*

as well as silk clothes. The fine variety of cloth is compared to the slough of the smoke, the foam of milk, and the cast off skin of a snake in Sangam classics. Pattinappalai mentions both of cotton and silk clothes.[315] Periplus praises the excellent quality of cloth produced by ancient Tamils, especially in Uraiyur. The varieties of cloth mentioned in *Cilappatikaram* may denote the improvements achieved since the early period of the Sangam age. In order to embellish the cloth, embroidery work was used.[316] Decorative motifs adorned the clothes and the dyeing also was prominent. *Porunar Arruppatai* reveals that fine silk dresses were in use.[317]

It was certain thft the spinning also might have been carried on in a large measure, otherwise there could be no weaving without yarn. Spinning needed much patience and hence it was generally entrusted with womenfolk, especially widows as they could be free from other domestic cares. The women continued spinning even late at night in the faint light of the oil lamps, and the women engaged in spinning were called 'paruttip pentir'.[318] All these things show that the people were engaged in spinning and weaving of cotton and silk which were profitable.

Toddy Tapping

During the Sang am age the toddy tapping also was an important occupation. Generally toddy was tapped from the spathe of palm trees. Toppi, a kind of toddy extracted from fermented grains of tinai or paddy also was common during the Sangam age.[319] *Pattinappalai* mentions various kinds of

315. Pattina. 107
316 Puram 274/1
317 Porunar. 155
318. Puram 376/5
319. Akam 35/9

today namely Pili,[320] mattu,[321] matu,[322] and naravu[323] and it explains that 'pili' was tapped from the spathe of palmyra tree. Toddy was generally known as 'kal'. The term 'teral' which denoted honey, also was used as a synonym for toddy.[324]

Some people of a particular group were exclusively engaged in toddy tapping and their womenfolk used to sell and they were called 'ariyal pentir'[325] perhaps this name might have been adopted from filtering the toddy by using the fibre of palm tree. Various kinds of toddy was freely distributed in the Royal courts and the bards were the recipients of a high class drink from the king. Invariably all the people of those days, whether men or women used to drink. It was also offered to 'natukal', the memorial stone, during worship, Hence the toddy tapping also was an important and profitable occupation of those days.[326]

Fishery

Fishing was an important occupation as it yielded much profit. The people who were engaged in fishing were called 'minavar' and 'valaiyari'. They used fishing-rod with the line and net for the purpose. They used to go into the far sea for fishing generally at night and return the next morning.[327] Pattinappalai says that 'paradavar' folk neglected their work on the full-moon day, as it was the auspicious day for Varuna, the sea-god.[328] They engaged themselves in pearl-fishing and

320. Pettina 89
321. *Ibid* 108
322. *Ibid* 108
323. *Ibid* 108
324. Puram 24/32
325. Akam. 57/17
326. Puram 232/3-4
327. Akam 65/11-12
328. Pattina. 92

collecting conch-shells,[329] which fetched a fair fortune. The fished were sold mostly at the spot (seashore) and then taken to the interior parts of the country. However they earned much by fishing and it was also an important occupation.

Salt Industry

Using the available natural resources some people at the coastal region were engaged in producing salt though it did not fetch them much profit. If the necessity of the commodity be considered, the salt should cost more but due to the availability in abundance, and the low cost of production, it was very cheap and the producer got only a marginal income. We learn from *Pattinappalai* that salt was sold in exchange of paddy which was used as a measure of value then and also that boats were used for the purpose. Further it reveals that ancient Tamils had used the rivers and canals for the transportation as far as possible. The people engaged in the salt trade were called 'umanar'.[330] Hence salt industry also was carried on as an occupation.

Trade

Pattinappalai provides ample scope for studying the extensive trade carried on those days in Tamilakam. It presents a panoramic view of the articles imported or exported at the Pukar port. However it introduced the trade with barter system. It portrays the boats came off with paddy got in barter of salt, and tied to the poles pitched in the back waters, which looked like the row of horses in a stable.[331] Other essential commodities also were sold in barter. Pedlars used to sell paddy,

329. Akam. 350/10-11
330. Puram. 313/5
331. Pattina. 29-31

millets, vegetables, liquor, etc. and occasionally clothes and ornaments too.

During the Sangam age the trade, both internal and foreign had been developed to a considerable extent. The exchange of essential commodities such as paddy, salt, vegetable, etc. on a barter basis "was common in those days, especially in villages. Side by side there were bazaars and markets in towns and cities, where the monetary system was prevalent. We learn from Sangam classics that the indigenous coins of Tamils were in use.[332] Generally the people sold the commodities produced by them to others in the neighbourhood and occasionally to those at a distance.

Sangam classics reveal that paddy and salt were used as a measure of value.[333] It is said that, in early days, the paddy and salt were given as wages. It is also said that the terms 'kuli' and 'campalam' which denote the wage, might have been derived from 'kulam' (grains) and 'alam' (salt-bed) respectively. The derivation 'kuli' from 'kulam' seems to be correct as even now paddy is given as wage for those who are employed in agriculture. But the next seems to be far-fetched and an appropriate.

Generally there were bazaars and markets in towns. The bazaar or market is mentioned in Sangam classics as 'ankati.'[334] There were 'nalankati'[335] (day bazaar) and 'allankati'[336] (evening or night bazaar). *Pattinappalai* mentions the market place as 'avanam'[337] and flags were flying in front of the shops indicating the sale of particular commodities,[338] and the poem

332. Akam. 369/8; Kuru. 67/4
333. Ibid. 60/4; Kuru. 269/5
334. Narrinai 258/7
335. Akam. 93/10
336. Cilampu. XXIII/150
337. paattina. 158
338. Ibid. Victuals 168; toddy 180

also mentions the sale of salt,[339] tasty victuals[340] fried fish and meat[341] and toddy.[342]

In those days there were only sandy tracks going from place to place; but passing through them was risky as there were wayside robbers,[343] So the merchants used to go in groups and the groups were called 'vanikaccaattu'.[344] Generally the bullock-carts were used for the purpose of transport but sometimes donkeys were also used for the purpose[345] of transport. The trunk roads connecting far off villages and towns were called 'peruvali'.[346] Tolls were collected at the entrance of the towns and at the junction of crossroads.[347]

There was no much scope for the trade through the inland -waterways of the country. The streams running through the hilly regions were thoroughly unfit for the purpose. Even the rivers running through plains were not useful due to periodical droughts arid floods. However the coastal waterways such as Buckingham canal and backwaters were useful to some extent. There are references in Sangam classics about the vessels used by ancient Tamils, namely, Punai,[348] pakri,[349] otam,[350] ampi,[351] and timil[352]. Timil was a small vessel which was used for fishing in the sea as well.

339. Ibid. 29
340. Ibid. 164
341. Ibid. 176-177
342. Ibid. 180
343. Akam. 89/10-13
344. Akam. 89½ 10-13
345. Ibid 39/10
346. perumpan. 80
347. Mullai. 97
348. Perumpan. 81
349. Kuru. 222/1-3
350. Akam. 101/12
351. Ainkuru. 98/2
352. Pattina. 112

It is certain that there was a well-developed maritime trade in Tamilakam during the Sangam age. Since the third century B.C., the Greeks became the carriers of the South Indian trade with the west. The expedition of Alexander and his finding of Alexandria provided the commercial expansion between South India and the West. After Julius Caesar the Romans succeeded the Greeks and took the trade with south India in their hands. After the conquest of Egypt, Agustus began to develop the trade with South India. Strabo says that 120 ships sailed to South India from Harmuz and he saw a Pandiyan embassy at the Royal court of Augustus. The discovery of the advantages of monsoon winds by Hippalus greatly increased the trade between South India and the West. There was a brisk trade in silk with China besides sugar. It is said that the word 'ceeni' for sugar may be a derivation from China-cina. Greeks and Romans came to Tamilakam as traders but soon arose many commercial colonies in Tamilakam. Greek merchants were called 'yavanas' first, subsequently it was applied to Romans, still later to all foreigners including the Arabs. The foreign merchants moved about the bazaars freely and transacted business. There might have been translators to help them in their transactions. We learn from Sangam classics that Mavilankai[353] Puraiyaru or Puruntai[354] and Pukar[355] were the important Cola ports of those days.

Pattinappalai presents a vivid picture of the pukar port with the articles either imported or to be exported. They are swift steeds brought by sea in ships;[356] Black pepper was brought by carts.[357] Gems and gold came from Himalayas.[358] (Probably this may mean the Vindhyas. Sandal and fragrant

353. Puram 176/6
354. Akam 100/13
355. Ibid 181/22; Puram 30/12
356. Pattina. 185
357. Ibid. 186
358. Ibid. 187

incense obtained from the eagle wood came from western ranges;[359] Pearls and red coral came from the southern and eastern seas respectively.[360] There came the yields of Ganges as well as of Kaviri[361] and precious things from Ceylon and rare manufactured things from Burma also arrived.[362] (The text line 191 reads as 'Ilattunavum' which means the food from ceylon is quite contrary to the reality. Hence it must be as 'Ilattulauum', which means the precious things from ceylon which is more probable and acceptable. Eminent scholars and commentators like Raghava lyengar and Somasundaranar are of the same view.)

We have to bear in mind that this vast trade was a great source of income to the Government by way of duties and tolls and hence it was the main source of country's economy. Considering all these above mentioned facts, it may be said that the economic, condition of the country was sound.

359. Ibid. 188
360. Ibid. 189
361. Ibid. 190
362. Ibid. 191

Chapter V

RELIGION

Pattinappalai provides a perfect conception of the various faiths followed by the people of the Sangam age. It speaks about the rustic form of Varunan worship by the fishermen folk as well as the civilized form of Murugan worship by the citizen of Pukar. It presents a vivid picture of the primitive form of kantu worship or the Linga worship of the early Tamils side by side with the Aryan form of worship through sacrifices performed by the sages with matted locks. Worship of Kali or Korravai the guardian Goddess of the city limits also has its legitimate place. Beyond all these things we see Pallis or the hermitages of the Jains and Buddhists.

The origin and its early activities of the religion is a problem yet to be solved, some are of opinion that fear might have been the basic factor for the religious impulse while some others argue that desire to achieve any particular object might have been the basic force. Ancestor worship in some form or other seems to be flourished in the early days and this might have been emerged as the hero-worship that is the worship of 'natukal or the memorial stone which is also known as 'virakkal' or hero stone. There are many references to this in the Sangam classics[363]. It is learnt that the hero-stones were decorated with peacock feathers and garlands,[364] and food and other things were offered.[365] A canopy of cloth also was put up over the hero stone,[366] and these stones were worshipped by the villagers as well as wayfarers.[367] We should bear in mind that this has nothing to do with the worship of 'kantu' or Linga worship.

Tolkappiyam reveals that Mayon (Tirumal), ceyon (Murukan), Ventan or Intiran and Varunan were the regional Gods of Mullai, Kurinci, Marutam and Neytal respectively[368]. However according to Sangam classics, the Murukan worship was predominant in almost all the regions. Though Korravai the Goddess of Palai or the desert region has no mention in *Tolkappiyam,* she is accepted as the goddess of war and victory by literature.

Mayon[369] was known as Mal[370] or Tirumal. There are six verses in *Paripatal* exclusively Intended for Tirumal. The term 'mal' means great and hence Tirumal may mean the great God. He is also known as Vishnu from which the term Vaishnavism was derived, but the word 'Vintu' instead of Vishnu is found in the Sangam literature.[371] This deity is referred to in Sangam classics such as *Purananuru, Paripatal, Kalittokai* and *Mullaippattu* as well as cilappatikaram. Krishna the incarnation of Vishnu is worshipped by all people who had accepted Vaishnavism. Madurai Kannattanar describes both Siva and Tirumal as the two great deities.[372]

363. Puram. 221/3
364. Ibid. 264/2-4; Akam 67/8-10
365. Ibid 329/1-4
366. Ibid, 260/25-29
367. Purapporul Venpa Malai 252
368. Tol. Akattinai Iyal 5
369. Paripatal 15/33
370. Ibid 13/6
371. Puram. 39/2
372. Akam 360/6

Siva

Siva is one of the great Gods of Tamils and some uphold that he is the supreme among them. The Tamils of the Sangam age considered Siva as one of the four supreme deities, the others being Murukan, Tirumal and Valiyon.[373] It is said that Murukan is the son of Siva, hence he is called as Cey or Ceyon [374] but he held primordial position among the other deities. During the Sangam age no doubt Siva held a secondary position to Murukan. Nakkirar describes these four as the props of universe.[375] It is said that Siva has an eye on his forehead[376] and hence He is known as Nerrikkannan or Mukkannan - the god of three eyes[377]. His favourite weapon is Trident.[378] Siva is also known as Nataraja on account of his dances which are called Kotukotti, Kapali and pantarankan. Although these dances belong to the Tamil conception they flourished only after the Sangam age. It was believed that due to the findings of Linga in large number and the Siva in the form of Pacupati at Harappa and Mohenjo-Daro, the Siva cult might have been closely connected with the Phallic cult. Invariably no temple of Siva will be without a Linga at the sanctum sanctorum of the temple and the Linga itself is called 'Sivalingam'.

There was a kantu in a large public hall called 'potiyil'[379] kept clean and decorated with flowers for public worship.[380] This potiyil was also called as Manram[381] and Ampalam.[382] It is believed during the Sangam age, the Linga worship was in the

373. Kali. 104/7-14
374. Tol. Akattinai lyal 5
375. Puram 56/1-10
376. Ibid. 55/4-5
377. Ibid. 6/18; Paripatal 5/29-30
378. Akam. Invocative verse, 5.
379. Puram. 52/12-13
380. Pattina. 249
381. Kuru. 15/2
382. Puram. 52 Commentary

form of Kantu worship. Naccinarkkiniyar explains that Kantu is a pillar in which God resides.[383] In some cases, the figure of the deity also was painted on the Kantu.[384] In course of time the idols and images might have been installed in the place of kantu.

Pattinappalai refers to Goddess Tirumakal.[385] In Sangam classics the term 'tiru' means Tirumakal (Lakshmi),[386] wealth[387], and beauty.[388]

Manimekalai mentions the Goddess as Ilakkumi.[389] She is said to be the wife of Mayon and goddess of wealth, prosperity, good fortunes as well as beauty, Kapilar an esteemed Sangam poet describes that Tirumakal seated on a lotus flower had been worshipped by elephants with water and flowers.[390]

There is a reference to the hermitages of Jains as well as Buddhists in *Pattinappalai*[391] and it shows that the followers of these faiths also were among the Tamils. According to Brahmi inscriptions found in the caverns of southern Tamilakam it is certain that Jains and Buddhists had entered Tamilakam before the second century B.C., There is a tradition that Bhadrabahu the Jain Saint followed by Chandragupta, the emperor, led a large number of his followers to Sravanabelagola as they were afraid of a serious famine in North India; but the identity of the saint and the emperor is not indisputably established. The second rock edict of Asoka reveals that hospitals for men and animals were established in the countries of Cola, Pandiya, Satyarputra, Keralaputra and

383. Pattina 249
384. Agam 167/15; Manimekalal XXI/1
385. Pattina. 41
386. Puram 358/6
387. Kuru, 181/6
388 Ibid.205/7
389. Manimekalai 7/108
390. Kalittokai 44/5-7
391. Pattina 53

Tampapanni (ceylon) and his thirteenth rock edict says that a mission to spread Buddhism had been sent to South India. Anyhow both Jainism and Buddhism had their followers in Tamilakam during the Sangam period. Many of the Jains had become great Tamil scholars and poets whose compositions are found in Sangam classiscs and Uloccanar may be taken as the best example. No doubt the Jains had done a marvellous service to the cause of Tamil and their contributions to the Tamil literature and grammar are very substantial.

Next we see the sages with matted looks, performing sacrifices,[392] and a little later we hear about the people who help the Brahmins to do their duties to Gods and offer oblations,[393] and protect cows and bulls, which are all indicating the Vedic or the Aryan influence in Tamilakam during the Sangam age. Sangam classics mention Yaga as Velvi[394] the sacrificial pillar as Yupam,[395] the oblation offered in the sacrificial fire as 'Neyppali'[396] and the priest who performed sacrifices as velvi antanar.[397] Many Tamil kings of that age took pride in performing Yagas, for instance, Rajasuyam vetta Perunarkilli, Palyagasalai Mutukutumi Peruvaluti and Palyanai Selkelu Kuttuvan may be mentioned. This will suffice to show how far the Tamils were influenced by the Vedic cult in the Sangam age.

Pattinappalai presents a pen-picture of the Varuna worship offered by the fishermen folk. The full moon day was an auspicious day to worship Varuna, the sea God. On that day the fishermen neglected fishing in the dark wide sea and erected a horn or sword of a gravid shark as a symbol of Varu-

392. Pattina. 54
393. Ibid. 200-202
394. Patirru. 64/4
395. puram 224/8
396. Ibid 15/19
397. Ibid 36/1

na and worshipped with offerings of food (meat and fish), and drink (toddy). Then they, with their black mates, ate and drank as well as they pleased and enjoyed company[398]. This can be the best example to show the religious activities of the rustic people of those days.

We have already seen the Murukan worship in connection with the veriyatu Makalir.

There we see a temple at the out skirt of Pukar. It is dedicated to Goddess Kali, the guardian of the city limits and it is not accessable as it is guarded by dreadful demons[399]. Kali is one of the village deities. It is believed that Kali and Korravai, the goddeas of Palai may be the same deity.

Ankalamman, Kaliamman, Mariyamman and Pitari are the dreadful village women deities. We can hear of the names such as Kaliappan and Kaliammal. This shows the people's faith in the Goddess. However we have to accept the existence of the village deities during the Sangam age.

There is a horrible sight also seen in *Pattinappalai.* In a captured town where once heard the pleasant music now the cruel jackals are bitterly whooping; and there are crowds of fearful goblins and the dreadful corpse-eating ghouls with dishevelled hair.[400]

The people of the Sangam age had a strong belief in ghosts and demons and numerous references are found in Sangam classics[401]. They were ferocious in their appearance with dishevelled hair and frightful eyes and they accepted offerings too[402]. They took delight in drinking the blood of the

398. Pattina 86-93
399. Ibid 57.
400. Ibid. 257-260
401. Puram 273/36; patirru. 23/37
402. Ibid 71/23-24

wounded and dead soldiers in the battle field and eating the corpses[403] and also in anointing their hair by the blood of the wounded soldiers[404]. This shows clearly the strong belief of the people of those days in ghosts and other evil spirits and how much they were afraid of such things.

The people of those days believed in life after death, which subsequently made them to follow the hero-worship with offerings. Gradually there arose the conception of Heaven[405] and Hell[406]. However they were afraid of the hell very much and used to take bath in the sea on auspicious days[407] to wash off their sins and thereby to escape from hell. The belief in omen and the dream and its effects also was popular among the people.

All these things can give us the various beliefs of the people of those days which were influenced by the religion they adopted.

---

403. Pattina. 126
404. Puram 62/2-3
405. Kalittokai 138/35; Maturaikkanci 197
406. Kuru. 258/65; Patirru. 15/31.
407. Pattina. 99

Chapter VI

ART AND CULTURE

Education

The value and importance of education were fully if realised by the Tamils of the Sangam age. *Tirukkural* provides an elaborate exposition of the value of learning, The Sangam classics show that education was popular among all classes of people as the poets invariably belong to different classes. The *Patinenkil kanakku* works indicate that educational activities had continued to be steady even after the Sangam age. Parents were keen in the education of their children. Ponmutiyar a Sangam poetess says that it is the duty of the father to educate and thereby ennoble his son[408]. *Pattinappalai* reveals that in Pukar, there were many eminent scholars who had hoisted flags so as to invite other great scholars for debate. This shows that education was much appreciated by all classes and hence there were many great scholars and poets. For example, the following names may be mentioned: Ilantevanar (merchant), Ilaveyinanar (hunter), Kaccilppettu ilantaccanar (carpenter), Tankal Porkollan Vennakanar (goldsmith), Nakkannaiyar (lady — merchant).

408. Puram 312/2

Literature

Literature may be considered as an autobiography of mankind. It portrays the life, thought and aspirations of the people concerned. The Sangam classics are of this kind. A striking feature of them is strict economy of words. There is no place for either religious or mythological ideas in them. The invocatory verses at the beginning of Tokai works were added later by the compilers. A distinctive feature of Sangam literature is as we have already seen the broad division of Akam and Puram and their various aspects. Generally a book should contain the fourfold aspects of human life that is Aram, Porul, Inpam and Vitu, but the last aspect is not stressed in Sangam classics.

Astrology and Astronomy

The poems of *Purananuru* show that the Tamils of Sangam age had acquired a fair knowledge of astrology. Kutalur Kilar says that on the Karthikai day of Pankuni, the people saw a star arose high above the sky and fell down into the water. They feared that a grave calamity would fall on the country. In fact, on the seventh day of the occurrence the king died[409]. This can be the best example for their knowledge of Astrology which was based on Astronomy.

Pattinappalai mentions the movements of the stars, planets as well as the moon. This shows that the early Tamils were able to differentiate the stars from the planets and the movements of the moon along with every asterism and the effects. There are too astronomical references in the text. The first is about the movement of the moon along with the asterism Makam which is formed by a group of four stars. It is said that a large tank with a temple on its bank, looks like

409. Puram. 229.

the full moon with Makam[410]. The agriculturist will observe the moon passing through the group of Makam on the full moon day of Maci, and from that they will assess the nature of harvest for the next year. The next reference is about the stars and planets. There was a wrestling contest witnessed by a large gathering. The participants were seen amidst the people and it looked like the ever bright planets amidst the numerous shining stars[411]. These references show cleanly that the Tamils of the Sangam age had acquired a fair knowledge of astrology and astronomy.

Music

The Tamils of the Sangam age had acquired a remarkable skill in music. They took great delight in enjoying music both vocal and instrumental. They were very much interested to witness either a dance performance or a play. This can be ascertained from the concept of 'muttamil' that is iyal, icai arid natakam.

Pattinappalai shows that the citizens of Pukar used to gather at a common place (probably a large hall) to enjoy music and witness dramas.[412] The term 'icai' itself denotes that the music will move or melt the minds of people. Whenever we think of Tamil music we have to think about the 'pan' the melody of Tamil icai. The Tamils of the sangam age were far advanced in music. They had separate pan for every region, namely kurincippan for Kurinci region,[413] pancuram for palai region,[414] catari for Mullai region,[415] marutappan for Maru-

410. Pattina. 35.
411. Ibid. 68.
412. Ibid. 113
413. Nampi Akapporul 20.
414. Ibid. 21.
415. Ibid. 22.

tam region[416] and cevvalippan for Neytal region.[417] In the same way they had separate Yal (stringed instrument) for the five & regions and they were called with the names of the respective regions, but vilari Yal for the neytal region. There were seven tunes Called kura, tuttarn, kaikkilai, ulal, ili, vilari and taram, each representing the seven strings of Yal. It was also restricted that a particular pan should be sung only in a particular time and there were appropriately adjusted musical tunes suited to various occasions such as marriage, religious functions, coronation or war.

Musical Instruments

There were numerous musical Instruments in Tamilakam. A poet who was well trained in various instruments was called Netumpalliyattanar.[418] *Pattinappalai* mentions about the kulal, yal, mulavu and muracu[419]. The most prominent kulal of the Sangam age is identified with the present flute. There were various types of yal. The mulavu (tabor) and the mulavu (drum) are the leather instruments. The muracu had played a prominent part in the royal activities. There are mentions about the tabor and lyre in lines 253 and 254 also.

These evidences show clearly that the Tamils of the Sangam age had acquired a remarkable skill in the field of music.

Dancing

In the Sangam period the dancing had attained a high degree of excellence and was cultivated with great enthusiasm.

416. Ibid. 23.
417. Ibid. 24.
418. Puram. 64
419. Pattina. 156-157

There were many kinds of dances such as *vallikkuttu, kura-vaikkuttu,* and so on. Our text refers to the veriyatal,[420] which was performed in honour of Lord Murukan. The art was well developed during the epic age and the dance performance exhibited by Matavi was quite different from those of vallik-kuttu etc., and far advanced. She received the Royal Award of 1008 kalancu pon which was the custom of those days.

Painting

The Tamils of the Sangam age paid proper attention to painting also. Sangam classics reveal that the figures of gods and natural sceneries were painted on the walls as well as on canvass. *Pattinappalai* refers to the painting of Goddess Tirumakal on the wall,[421] and the tiger, the royal emblem on the doors[422]. It also hints about the various figures painted on the walls[423]. It is sure that there might have been literature on painting. *Manimekalai* mentions about 'oviyac cennul'[424]. It says that the painter will create the figure to draw in his mind first then draw it and finally paint it[425]. The unpainted drawing was called '*Punaiya Oviyam*'[426]. The painting, in Tamil, was called 'oviyam' and the painter was called 'oviyam'.

Hospitality

Hospitality was a marked virtue of the ancient Tamils from time immemorial. *Tirukkural* describes this virtue in detail. Hospitality was considered as an essential duty of a householder, and hence they gave a warm welcome to their guests

420. Ibid. 155
421. Ibid. 41
422. bid. 40
423. Ibid 49.
424. Manimekalai 2/31
425. Ibid. 5/7
426. Netunal. 147

and provided delicious meals with much enthusiasm. Cordiality to neighbours also was considered as a duty of a householder.

Malaipatukatam narrates how the hosts hurried to welcome their guests in such a manner, a man rushed to rescue a drowning man. They invited their guests warmly and used to share their food with them (guests)[427]. Even if the guests came late at night they were sure to get meal and shelter.[428] Charity was an allied virtue of the ancient Tamils; feeding the poor was believed to be a sacred duty. Hence the ancient Tamils were more hospitable and charitable.

Pattinapalai provides ample scope for these things. There were public halls called 'potiyil' or 'manram' or 'ampalam', where 'kantu' the God's emblem was erected for worship. The local people would come, worship and go, but the new comers from other places, who came late in the evening, used to worship and stay there for the night, and the bright lamps would be burning throughout night[429]. There were public feeding houses in Pukar and the large quantity of 'kanci' the rice water drained from the cooked rice, was flowing through the street like a rivulet[430]. There were kitchen halls where numerous people were fed and the surplus meals was kept ready for the new comers.[431] Besides all these, the foreigners who had diverse tongues, stayed in Pukar on trade purposes, led a free and happy life as they received kind hospitality from the Tamils.

The fishes moved about freely near the houses of fishermen and cattle fearlessly roamed about the front of the hous-

427. Pattina. 280-286
428. Puram. 317
429. Pattina 247-249
430. Ibid. 43-45
431. Ibid. 261-262

es of butchers. The people of Pukar condemned taking off these lives and hated stealing totally[432]. This kind of toleration and good behaviour besides their kind hospitality show their well developed culture.

In view of the facts we have seen so far, it is clear that education was popular among all people and poets represented almost all communities. The fine arts such as music, dance and drama as well as painting were well developed furring the Sangam age. Hospitality shown by the Tamils was the best example to show their renowned culture.

432. Ibid. 197-199.

Chapter VII

CONCLUSION

The foregoing chapters of this Book contain a critical and analytical study of Pattinapalai, one of the ten idylls. This poem provides cope for the study of the political, social, economic, cultural and religious life of the Tamils during the Sangam age. It gives us an account of the early heroic achievements of Tirumavalavan and the succeeding successful military exploits as well as his benevolent rule. He was a merciless military genius. It portrays Pukar the capital city and its massive mansions by the side of the wide bazaars filled with various kinds of flags; and the very busy harbour with international trade.

According to the nature and style of the language used and the matter contained in the collection of Pattuppattu, it is clear that this collection should be a composition of a later date to other Sangam classics - that is the Eight Anthologies.

The political conditions of Tamilakam during the reign of Tirumavalavan, was steady and balanced as he was an absolute and mighty monarch in Tamilakam. In his early clays itself, he thoroughly defeated his agnate enemies and got back his kingdom. Soon after this heroic victory he began his military exploits. He subdued all the neighbour states around his kingdom and annexed them to his empire; and no one dared to rise against him. Even the Pandiyan king was scared by his victories. This must be the main cause for the statement of Ilanko Atikal that Tirumavalavan had led his military expedition upto Himalayas and imprinted his royal-emblem the tiger mark on it and returned, and such was his victorious military exploits. No doubt he was a great warrior among the Tamil king Trio then and a builder of the vast Colas empire. Hence his subjects enjoyed a perfect and peaceful life, which enabled them to have a prospective career of life. We have to bear in mind that Tontaiman Ilantiraiyan, the patron of *Perumpanarruppatai* was a contemporary to Tirumavalavan, the patron of *Pattinappalai* as Uruttirankannanar himself is the author of that poem also and both poems were composed in the life time of the patrons.

We see the social order of the country next. Pukar being a coastal city the poem speaks about the marutam and neytal regions only and hence the agriculturists, merchants and paratavar are shown as the major communities. We see yavanas the foreign merchants too among the citizens of Pukar. Incidentally the Brahmins also appear to receive help from the Ulavar community to do their daily duties and religious rites as well. Their usual food and drink are spoken in detail to some extent. It is clear that cotton and silk dresses with various ornaments were in use then, and we hear about the garments of foliage (talai) used by the womenfolk of paratavar community. A sceneray of a wrestling match among the rustic population is beautifully described. The elites of the capital city were indulged in listening music, enjoying dances and witnessing dramas as their pastime activities. Artists such as painters, dancers (veriyatu makalir) musicians and players on musical instruments such as flute and lute as well as drum and tabor are also given their due places. On the whole it presents a fine pen-picture of the social order prevailed during the Sangam age.

Pattinappalai depicts a comprehensive but a vivid picture of the economic condition of the ancient Tamils. The country's economy was mainly based on agriculture and trade, cultivation of paddy and sugarcane was the most important occupations of the people and fishing gets the next place representing marutam and neytal respectively. Sugarcane presses were found here and there and sugar industry also was progressive. Weaving also was one of the main occupations of the people. This poem provides us with full information about trade and commerce both inland and foreign carried on by the ancient Tamils. It furnishes a long list of articles and goods, arrived at the port either imported or to be exported, and the harbour looks like a great emporium of South India. The customs officials were very vigilant in guarding the goods as well as in collecting the duties. Tolls and duties also were one of the main sources of income to the Royal treasury. We see flags flying in front of every shop indicating the articles sold and quoting the prices too. The merchants were fair and just in their dealings and openly announced their profits, such was the honesty and magnanimity of merchants of those days. In all respects the economic condition of the people was sound.

Pattinappalai graphically shows the advancement in fine arts and culture among the Tamils, during the Sangam age. The common people of Pukar were engaged in celebrating the Murukan festivals with 'veriyatal' (dance) accompanied by music and musical instruments such as flute and lyre as well as tabor and drum. More civilized and well-to-do people spent their leisure time by attending the music and dance performances and witnessing the plays as well. The Tamils of those days were well renowned for their hospitality.

Religion is an inseparable and the most important factor in human life. This aspect of the Tamils is categorically described in Pattinappalai. We see the worship of 'kantu' in a well decorated and lighted large hall called 'potiyil'. This is considered to be the earliest form of worship in which the 'kantu' was meant to be God's emblem. At the next stage we hear about the worship of Lord Murukan, which seems to be the predominant God of Tamils through the ages. The author takes us to witness a festival celebrated in honour of Murukan, with 'veriyatal' in the wide street of Pukar and also the maids who offer their prayers with folded hands. Then he leads us to the seashore where the paratavar folk offer their prayers to Varuna the sea-God; by erecting a decorated shark-horn as a symbol of the deity.

Incidentally we see the hermitages of Jains and Buddhists who were the recent guests to Tamilakam then, and also we meet the sages with matted locks performing sacrifices which proclaims the acceptance of the Aryan cult by the Tamils. Finally we see the temple dedicated to Kali a village deity, guarded by the frightful demons, being a note to the acceptance of village deities during the Sangam age itself and the belief in ghosts and demons and evil spirits.

The facts we have seen so far prove it clearly that *Pattinappalai* is one of the most reliable sources of the history of the Tamils of the Sangam age.

BIBLIOGRAPHY

Sangam Classics

1. Ainkurunuru, Dr. U.V.S. Iyer Edn., Madras, 1944.
2. Akananuru, Chakravarthy Rajagopalachari, Madras, 1935.
3. Cilappatikaram, Dr. U.V.S. Iyer Edn., Madras, 1927.
4. Cirupanarruppatai, Dr. U.V.S. Iyer Edn., Madras, 1931.
5. Kalittogai, S.I.S.S.P. Works, Madras, 1938.
6. Kuruntogai, Dr. U.V.S. Iyer Edn., Madras, 1937.
7. Malaipatukatam, Dr. U.V.S. Iyer Edn., Madras, 1931.
8. Manimekalai, Dr. U.V.S. Iyer Edn., Madras, 1931.
9. Maturaikkanci, Dr. U.V.S. Iyer Edn., Madras, 1931.
10. Mullaipattu, Dr. U.V.S. Iyer Edn., Madras, 1931.
11. Nalatiyar. S.I.S.S.P. Works Edn, Madras, 1945.
12. Narrinai, Narayanasami Iyer Commentary, Madras Rakshasa Year.
13. Netunalvatai, Dr. U.V.S. Iyer Edn., Madras, 1931.
14. Palamoli, S.I.S.S.P. Works Edn, Madras, 1948.
15. Paripatal, Dr. U.V.S. Iyer Edn., Madras, 1935.
16. Patirrupattu, Dr. U.V.S. Iyer Edn., Madras, 1941.
17. Pattinapalai, Dr. U.V.S. Iyer Edn., Madras, 1931.
18. Perumpanarruppatai, Dr. U.V.S. Iyer Edn., Madras, 1931.
19. Porunararruppatai, Dr. U.V.S. Iyer Edn., Madras, 1931.

20. Purananuru, Dr. U.V.S. Iyer Edn., Madras, 1935.
21. Tirukkural, S.I.S.S.P. Works Edn, Madras, 1937.

Works in Tamil

1. Appar, *"Tevaram"*, Samajam Edn., Madras, 1941.
2. Cekkilar, *"Tiruttontar Puranam"*, Samajam Edn., Madras.
3. Ceyankontar, *"Kalinkattup parani"*, A. V. Cunniah Naidu, Madras, 1941.
4. Govindan, K., *"Canka Kala Aracar Varical"*, S.I.S.S.P. Works, Madras, 1961.
5. Govindan K., *"Trumavalavan"*, S.I.S.S.P. Works, Madras, 1939.
6. Iraiyanar, *"Akapporul"*, Bhavanandar Kazhagam, Madras, 1939.
7. Maraimalai Atigal, *"Pattinappalai Araycci Urai"*, S.I.S.S.P. Works, Madras, 1957.
8. Nakaviraca Nampi, *"Akapporul"*, S.I.S.S.P. Works, Madras, 1958.
9. *"Panniru Pattiyal"*, S.I.S.S.P. Works, Madras, 1943.
10. Raghava Iyengar, *"Pattinappalai Araycci"*, Annamalai University, 1951.
11. Rajamanicakam, M., *"Critical Study in Pattuppattu"*, University of Madras, 1970.
12. Sadasiva Pandarattar, T.V., *"Tamil Ilakkiya Varalaru* (250-600 A. D.)", Annamalai
13. University, 1957.
14. Tolkappiyar, *"Tolkappiyam"*, Porulatikarara, S. Kanagasabapati Piliai Edn.,
15. Madras, 1934.
16. Vaiyapuri Piliai, S., *"Iiakkiyac Cintanaikal"*, Star Piracuram, Madras, 1947.

Works in English

1. Arokiaswami, M., *"The Classical Age of the Tamils"*, University of Madras, Reprinted, 1972.
2. Chelliah, J.V., *"Pattupattu"*, S.I.S.S.P. Works, 1962, Madras.
3. Kanagasabal V., *"Tamil Eighteen Hundred Years Ago"*, Higginbothams & Co., Madras, 1904.
4. Jesudasan, C., *"History of Tamil Literature"*, YMCA Publishing House, Calcutta, 1961.
5. Majumdar, R.C., *"History and Culture of the Indian People"*, Vol. IV, 1960.
6. Meenakshi sundaram Piliai T. P., *"A History of Tamil Literature"*, Annamalai University, 1965.
7. Nilakanta Sastri, K.A., *"Comprehensive History of India"*, Vol. II, 1956.
8. Nilakanta Saatri, K.A., *"Foreign Notices of South India"*, University of Madras, 1972.
9. Nilakanta Sastri, K.A., *"History of South India"*, Oxford University Press, Madras, 1955.
10. Nilakanta Saatri, K.A., *"The Cholas"*, Vol. I, University of Madras, 1936.
11. Nilakanta Sastri, K.A., *"The Pandyan Kingdom"*, Luzao & Co., Madras, 1929.
12. Pillay K.K., *"A Social History of the Tamils"*, Vol. I, University of Madras, 1975.
13. Purnalingam Pilial, M.S., "History of Tamil Literature", Madras.
14. Ramachandra Dikshitar, V. R., *"Studies in Tamil Literature and History"*, University of Madras, 1936.
15. Ramachandran, C.E., "Ahananuru in its History Setting", University of Madras, 1974.
16. Ramachandran, C.E., "*Tirumavalavan*", Journal of the Madras University, Vol. 34. No. 1. 1-7-1962.

17. Sivaraja Pillai K.N., *"Chronology of the. Early Tamils",* University of Madras, 1932.
18. Smith, V. A., *"Early History of India",* 1957.
19. Srinivasa lyengar, M., *"Tamil Studies",* Madras Guardian Press, Madras, 1914.
20. Srinivasa lyengar, P.T., *"History of the Tamils",* C. Coomara Swamy Naidu & Son's, Madras, 1929.
21. Subramanian H., *"Sangam Polity",* Ennes Publication, 1980.
22. Subramanian H., *"History of the Tamil Nad",* Koodal Publishers, Madurai, l972.

INDEX

D

E

F

G

H

I

R

S

T

U

V

www.ingramcontent.com/pod-product-compliance
Lightning Source LLC
LaVergne TN
LVHW011403080426
835511LV00005B/394